EDUCATION OF EXCEPTIONAL CHILDREN

M. DASH

ATLANTIC
PUBLISHERS & DISTRIBUTORS (P) LTD

Published by

ATLANTIC

PUBLISHERS & DISTRIBUTORS (P) LTD

7/22, Ansari Road, Darya Ganj,
New Delhi-110002
Phones : +91-11-40775252, 23273880, 23275880, 23280451
Fax : +91-11-23285873
Web : www.atlanticbooks.com
E-mail : orders@atlanticbooks.com

Branch Office
5, Nallathambi Street, Wallajah Road,
Chennai-600002
Phones : +91-44-64611085, 32413319
E-mail : chennai@atlanticbooks.com

Printed in India at Glorious Printers, A-13, D.S.I.D.C.,
Jhilmil Industrial Area, Delhi-110095

Preface

At some time or other, practically all school teachers will have exceptional children in their classrooms. These individuals are important members of the human community. It is realised now that special education can no longer remain as the exclusive domain of special educators. Meeting the special needs of children with exceptionality is the shared responsibility of regular classroom teacher, resource teachers, therapists, psychologists and other members of the education team which also includes the parents.

Teacher education programmes in various Institutes of Advanced Studies in Education, Colleges of Teacher Education, District Institutes of Education and Training and University Department of Education have been reoriented to equip teacher-trainees and inservice teachers with the knowledge and skills required to manage the exceptional children in the regular classrooms. My objective in writing this introductory textbook is to assist teachers to understand the children with exceptionality, to develop a positive view and a rational attitude towards these children and their special needs and organise appropriate programmes of education and other related services for them, the main thrust being : A teacher has to help the bud into full bloom and not to make paper flowers to satisfy his whim.

In preparing the manuscript I was influenced by what I learned in Moray House College of Education, Edinburgh, my interaction with resource teachers and regular teachers of Orissa in various training programmes on IEDC, faculty members of various Indian Universities and NCERT during my training in Special Education and Integrated Education, the feedback received from my B.Ed. students, my own administrative experiences in Centrally Sponsored Scheme of IEDC, and particularly some outstanding literature on education of exceptional children a list of which has been given at the end of this book. I am grateful to all those who have shaped my thinking directly or indirectly and particularly to the great publishers and authors whose books have helped me tremendously in finding out, summarizing, incorporating the latest findings in the field of special education and integrated education for children with exceptionalities. I am particularly grateful to Dr. K.R. Gupta, Managing Director, M/s Atlantic Publishers and Distributors, New Delhi for publishing this book.

I will welcome and appreciate comments and suggestions, if any, from my readers for improving the book in subsequent editions.

MURALIDHAR DASH

CONTENTS

1

The Concept of Exceptional Children

1. Who are the Exceptional Children?

In a democratic country like ours every child has the right to education — the right to receive help in learning to the limits of his capacity, whether that capacity be small or great. It is consistent with a democratic philosophy that all children be given equal opportunity to learn whether they are average, bright, dull, retarded, blind, deaf, crippled, delinquent, emotionally disturbed or otherwise limited or deviant in their capacities to learn. Equality of opportunity denotes two things — equality of access to school education and equality of success in school.

In every classroom there are some children who have some learning problems. They need a little extra help from teachers to learn. Sometimes teachers understand their problems while at other times they are not able to understand their problems. The help they provide may not be sufficient. Their learning problems may persist and even accumulate despite special help by teachers. If teachers cannot understand the special needs of such children they will experience failure and frustration and later drop out from the school. In fact our failure to understand the special needs of such children have been major factors for our failure to reach the target of universalization of elementary education within the stipulated period. These children with special needs are called exceptional.

The term 'exceptional' means different things to different people. Some use it when referring to the particularly bright children or the child with unusual talent. Others use it when they refer to any typical or deviant child. Telford and Sawrey (1972) said, "To be exceptional is to be rare or unusual."

Kirk (1962) defines an exceptional child as "that child who deviates from the average or normal child in mental, physical, or social characteristics to such an extent that he requires a modification of school practices, or special educational services in order to develop to his maximum capacity."

Cruickshank (1974) also holds similar view when he defines an exceptional child as "a child who deviates intellectually, physically, socially, or emotionally so much from what is considered to be normal growth and development that he cannot receive maximum benefit from regular school programme and requires a special class or supplementary instruction and services."

Hewett and Forness (1984) have given a comprehensive definition of exceptional learner : "An exceptional learner is an individual who, because of uniqueness in sensory, physical, neurological, temperamental or intellectual capacity and/or in the nature and range of previous experience, requires an adaptation of the regular school programme in order to maximize his or her functioning level." All children traditionally labeled as exceptional fall under this definition.

An analysis of these definitions indicates the following facts about the exceptional child :

(i) The exceptional child is one who is waiting to be taught in right direction with suitable methods and materials in a suitable environment and with right spirit.

(ii) The exceptional child is a unique child. His uniqueness may be noticed in one or more of the following dimensions — vision, hearing, movement, perceptual-motor, communication, social-emotional and intelligence. Thus, the blind, deaf, crippled, learning disabled, speech handicapped, emotionally disturbed, socially disadvantaged, mentally retarded, slow learner and the gifted children are exceptional.

(iii) The uniqueness of the exceptional child may be also noticed in the amount and quality of previous experiences received in the home.

(iv) The uniqueness of the child may be in the negative direction (as in case of handicapped children) or in the positive direction (as in case of gifted and creative children).

(v) Contrary to the popular view, the exceptional child has potential for growth and learning. But he cannot profit from the regular school programme.

(vi) He requires modification or adaptation of school practices, special education and other related services in order to maximize his functioning level.

(vii) The disabled, disadvantaged, disturbed and the gifted children are exceptional children. Recently such children are called "children with special needs."

2. Positive and Negative Deviations

Children are unique. If we survey a busy playground we see a spectacle of this uniqueness. Some children move more quickly and with better coordination than others. Some children are surrounded by admiring friends whereas others sit alone at some distance. The differences we observe on the playground are more obvious than those we might see inside the classroom. The field of special education is concerned with children who deviate from normal children to the extent that matters very much for learning in schools and functioning successfully elsewhere. There are seven critical dimensions related to successful learning in school and successful adaptation elsewhere. These seven dimensions are — vision, hearing, movement, communication, perceptual-motor, social-emotional and intelligence. An exceptional child deviates from normal children on any one dimension or more either in positive direction or in negative direction.

Vision : The dimension of vision is critical with respect to instruction in the classroom and free, independent movement through the environment. We all vary visually. Some of us who have excellent vision and can see farther and more clearly than most deviate from the normal individuals in the positive direction. Many of us fall around the mid-point of the vision dimension. Those who wear corrective lenses, those who have visual problems and the blind deviate from the normal individuals in the negative direction. Again those who deviate in the negative direction fall at varying points within this range.

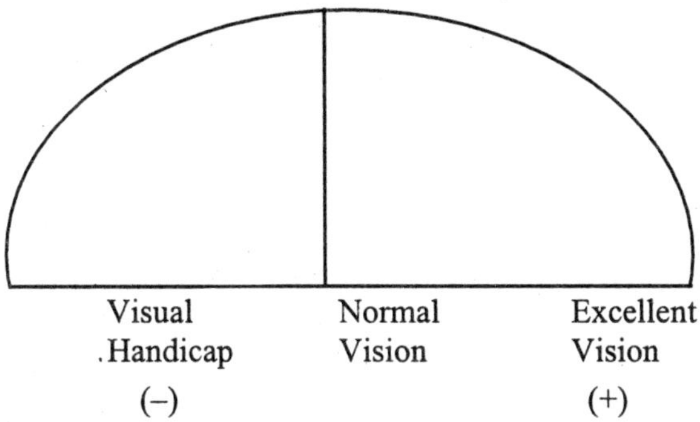

Hearing : Another dimension very critical to learning is hearing. Some of us who deviate from the normal individuals in positive direction have acute hearing and are able to detect even the faintest sound at a distance of more than 250 feet. Most of us fall near the middle on the hearing dimension. Some of us who deviate from the normal individuals in the negative direction experience difficulties in hearing. Those who deviate in the negative direction have varying degrees of hearing loss and need varying degrees of amplification provided by a hearing aid. Even some fall far down the problem range and are deaf.

Profound Hearing Loss	Severe Hearing Loss	Moderate Hearing Loss	Mild Hearing Loss	Normal Hearing	Acute Hearing
(–)					(+)

Movement : Some of us may function far up in the positive range on the movement dimension like the gifted athletes. Most of us are likely at mid-point. Some of us deviate in the negative direction and have problems of movement unless provided with braces or a wheel chair. Even some are completely immobilized and are confined to their beds. The orthopaedically handicapped, children with cerebral palsy or crippling conditions deviate from the normal in the negative direction.

Perceptual-Motor : The perceptual-motor dimension is concerned with how accurately we perceive stimuli in our environment and respond to them. Some of us have no problems in recognizing, speaking, reading, writing or understanding words and numbers. The learning disabled children have difficulty in speaking or reading or writing or using numbers or comprehending facts. Some learning disabled children may perceive everything visually as upside down and backwards. Such children may have minimal brain dysfunction.

Communication : Communication is very essential in every day life and for learning in school. Some individuals are very positive and communicate freely and accurately using the right vocabulary and structural patterns at the right moment. Some of us, however, have difficulty in communicating with others. Individuals with stuttering, stammering and articulation problems deviate from the normal individuals in the negative direction in the communication dimension.

Social-Emotional : The social-emotional dimension has to do with how well we get along in our day-to-day living, particularly how well we relate to others. Some of us are real winners. Some of us are loved, respected, sought out, surrounded by admiring friends, and happy. Others manage to get by. Some of us are emotionally stable and socially matured. Some children display problem behaviour in some situations and not in others. But some children like the delinquents, emotionally disturbed and particularly the autistic children, fall at the extreme end of the negative range along this dimension.

Intelligence : Intelligence is such a dimension along which both the positive and the negative directions are of concern to teachers and administrators. In the positive range we have individuals with superior intelligence — the gifted ones. In the negative range we have mentally retarded individuals. In each direction individuals fall at varying positions in terms of IQ ranges. For example, mentally retarded individuals who deviate from the normal individuals in the negative direction may be mildly retarded (IQ 55-70), moderately retarded (IQ 40-54), severely retarded (IQ 25 to 39) or profoundly retarded (IQ below 25). In school situation children having IQ 50 to 75 are educable mentally retarded, children having IQ 25 to 50 are trainable mentally retarded, and children having IQ below 25 are custodial mentally retarded. Children who deviate from the normal either in the positive direction or in the negative direction are exceptional so far as school learning is concerned.

3. Concepts of Impairment, Disability and Handicap

In the field of special education the three terms *Impairment, Disability*, and *Handicap* are very often used interchangeably. Thus, we come across expressions like hearing-impairment, hearing-disability, and hearing-handicap to refer to hearing loss. These three terms actually mean different things.

An impairment is a permanent or transitory psychological, or anatomical loss and/or abnormality. This may be so from birth, or acquired later. Example : a hole in the ear drum, a missing or defective part of the body, paralysis after polio, myopia, low level of intelligence, etc.

Impairment may cause functional limitations. Functional limitation means partial or total inability to perform those activities necessary for motor, sensory or mental functions within the range and manner of which a human being is normally capable such as walking, lifting loads, seeing, speaking, hearing, reading, writing, taking interest in and making contact with surroundings. A functional limitation may last for a short time, be permanent or reversible. Limitations may be progressive or regressive.

Impairment leads to disability. Disability is defined as an existing difficulty in performing one or more activities which are generally accepted as essential components of daily living. Due to the impairment there is a reduction in functional ability. For example, due to the hole in the ear drum, the child is unable to hear normally. A visually impaired child cannot see properly because of faulty image formation. An orthopaedically handicapped child cannot use the arms and fingers for gripping. A learning disabled child cannot calculate or understand number relationships like a normal child. Depending in part on the duration of the functional limitation disability may be short-term, long-term, or permanent.

Medically, disability is physical impairment and inability to perform physical functions normally. Legally, disability is a permanent injury to body for which the person should or should not be compensated. Disability can be divided into three periods :

(i) Temporary total disability,

(ii) Temporary partial disability,

(iii) Permanent disability.

Temporary total disability is that period in which the affected person is totally unable to work. During this time he may receive orthopaedic, optalmological, auditory or speech or any other medical treatment. Temporary partial disability is that period when recovery has reached the stage of improvement so that the person may begin some kind of gainful occupation. Permanent disability refers to permanent damage to or loss of some parts of the body even after any medical treatment.

Just as impairment leads to disability, disability handicaps the individual. Handicap means a restriction imposed/acquired by the child's disability which affects the efficiency of his/her day-to-day life activities. The term handicap refers to the problems a person with a disability or impairment encounters in interacting with the environment. A disability may pose a problem in one environment but not in another. The child with an artificial limb may be handicapped when competing against non-disabled peers in a football match but experiences no handicap in the classroom. Thus, a disabled person is not handicapped, however, unless the physical disability leads to educational, personal, social, vocational, or other problems. The handicapping effects of a disability can be reduced by corrective services like hearing aids, artificial limbs, medical interventions, etc.

The differences between these three terms can be summarized as follows : Impairment is structural, disability is functional and handicap is social-psychological.

4. Types of Exceptional Children

Exceptional children are of various types such as the following :

(i) Children with Hearing Handicap

(ii) Children with Visual Handicap

(iii) Children with Mental Retardation

(iv) Children with Learning Disability

(v) Children with Orthopaedic Handicap

(vi) Children with Emotional Disturbance

(vii) Children with Speech Handicap

(viii) Children with Special Health Problems
(ix) Children with Multiple Handicaps
(x) Gifted Children
(xi) Children with Creative Talents
(xii) Socially Disadvantaged Children

A brief discription of these children is given below :

Children with Hearing Handicap : The hearing handicapped are those children who have a damaged hearing mechanism and face difficulty in speech and language development. There is loss of hearing. The degree of hearing loss is less in some children while it is more severe in others. The hearing handicapped children may be hard-of-hearing or deaf.

The hard-of-hearing children are those children who have hearing loss but who can hear if spoken too loudly without a hearing aid. A hearing aid will enable them to hear better. For such children education in general schools in common with other children is not difficult. Most of them are already studying in the general classroom.

The deaf are those who cannot hear even if spoken to very loudly. They require preparation in basic skills through special techniques before they are admitted in general schools. Hearing aids help them to become more functional.

Children with hearing impairment need hearing aid, auditory training, more of visual cues in the teaching-learning situation, services of audiologist, ENT specialists, special education and other supportive aids and services. The special needs of such children differ depending upon the type and nature of hearing loss, the quality of previous training received in the home and pre-school centres etc.

Children with Visual Handicap : The visually handicapped children are those who have problems with vision. Some visually handicapped children can read large print and are functional in their environment whereas some have severe vision loss and cannot be taught through visual methods. The visual loss is measured with the help of Snellen Chart. Depending upon the degree of loss they may be partially sighted or blind.

The partially sighted are those who require large print or magnified print materials. Their visual acquity (sharpness of visual image) is very low (20/70 in the better eye). This means that the child can see at 20 ft. distance what a normal child sees at 70 ft. Their eye-sight may be weak due to short sightedness, long sightedness, astigmatism, glaucoma or muscle detachment.

The blind are those who need to be taught through braille or through aural method. Their visual acquity (sharpness of visual image) may fall at 2/200. Such children must be prepared in pre-academic skills like braille reading, braille writing and use of cane for mobility before they are admitted in general schools. They need orientation training, mobility training and more of oral instruction depending upon the degree of loss of vision.

Childern with Mental Retardation : Mentally retarded children are those who have a lower level of intellectual functioning and have problems in social adaptability. There are various degrees of mental handicap. Consequently there are various categories of mentally handicapped children — the educable mentally retarded (EMR), the trainable mentally retarded (TMR) and the custodial mentally retarded (CMR).

The educable mentally retarded are those who have minimum educational retardation in school subjects. Such children have problems of social adjustment, but are usually not recognised as mentally retarded at the pre-school level. They need repetition of instruction. The adaptive behaviours of such children should be observed carefully by the teachers so that they can be identified in the early stages.

The trainable mentally retarded can be trained in vocational areas. They are poor in adaptive behaviour and may need training in daily living skills at the initial levels.

The custodial mentally retarded need help in developing daily living skills. They can be educated in special institutions/special classes. They are very poor in adaptive behaviour. They need constant care and attention.

Children with Learning Disability : These children are like other children in intellectual functioning. They are not mentally retarded, nor do they have visual or hearing problems. But they have problems in spelling, reading, writing, arithmetic, listening and comprehension. Their problem may be due to cerebral dysfunction/emotional/behavioural disturbance, but it is not due to mental retardation, sensory handicap or instructional practices. Depending upon the degree of disability such children may be categorised into mild learning disabled and severe learning disabled.

Such children have a severe discrepancy between their achievement and intellectual ability. Such children may have the following specific problems :

Reading disability

Writing disability

Problems in comprehension and communication

Problems in numerical ability.

Such children need repetition and drill, cognitive modelling, process training, multisensory experiences and remedial instruction.

Children with Speech Handicap : Speech handicap refers to minor and major speech and language problems. There are children with mild language and speech disorders in our classrooms, and they often go unnoticed. While speaking and writing they tend to omit, distort, add or substitute words, phrases, letters of the alphabet etc. They stammer and are quiet or have long gaps in speaking full sentences. Their problems should be corrected before they start school. The major types of speech disorders are :

voice disorders,
articulation or pronunciation disorders, and
fluency disorders.

Children with Special Health Problems : Under this category we have children whose poor physical condition makes them inactive and who require special health precautions in school and adequate medical check-ups and support. Such children can be categorised into two groups :

Children with mild health problems, and
Children with severe health problems.

Epilepsy, diabetic problems, asthma, pain in the joints and anaemia are some of the special health handicaps.

Children with Multiple Handicaps : Multiple handicap refers to more than one handicap in the child. A child may be blind and deaf, blind and orthopaedically handicapped, deaf and orthopaedically handicapped, mentally retarded and orthopaedically handicapped and so on. In case of multiple handicap one handicap may be primary handicap and the other secondary or one handicap may be more severe than the other handicaps. It is, therefore, important to identify the primary handicap and take measures accordingly. Such children need intensive medical care, superior instruction from the teacher and a little love and affection from the parents and teachers.

Children with Orthopaedic Handicap : Some children have orthopaedic handicap or locomotor handicap. Locomotor handicap refers to problems with the functioning of bones, joints and muscles. In some cases the problems are so severe that they require artificial limbs to compensate for their crippling conditions. In other cases they need wheel chair or crutches. They need removal of architectural barriers and some environmental modifications in the school. Usually mildly orthopaedically handicapped children do not have learning problems. They can be integrated in the regular school without much difficulty.

Children with Emotional Disturbance : Children with emotional disturbance are very often considered as problem children in the school. An emotionally disturbed child has certain inner tensions which create anxiety, frustration, fears and impulsive behaviour. Such a child may find excuses for his inner tensions in some physical difficulty. An emotionally disturbed child may attempt to solve the anxiety by behaving in a premature or childish way, becoming aggressive towards other people, or withdrawing himself to the world of fantasy. Such children need love and protection, security and recognition, pleasant and success experiences in the home and the school.

Gifted Children : Gifted children are in some way superior in intellectual ability to other children of the same age. Gifted children are those who have demonstrated high ability (including high intelligence), high creativity and high task commitment — a high level of motivation and the ability to see a project through to its conclusion. A variety of terms have been used to describe individuals who are superior in some way such as 'talented', 'creative', 'genius', and 'precacious' (remarkably early development in particular areas like language, music, mathematical ability). Most of these children remain unidentified in the class. Specific efforts are also not made to meet the special needs of such children. Such children who do not profit much from the regular school programme need early admission in schools, skipping grades, telescoping grades, early admission in secondary schools and colleges and enrichment activities and materials.

Children with Creative Talents : In a school teachers may come across few students who have the ability to produce something new — a composition, a system of ideas or a material or a process which is essentially new or novel, and previously unknown to them. Such children behave differently. They are courageous in their convictions. They have independent thinking and adjustment. They become absorbed and preoccupied in what they are doing. They are curious. They take risks. They are flexible in their opinions. They are intellectually self-confident. The prevailing school practices and situations create hindrance for their creative expressions. Teachers need to modify their attitudes towards such children and employ suitable strategies for promotion of their creativity.

Socially Disadvanted Children : Most teachers encounter a group of children in their classrooms who appear lifeless, incurious, and deceptively unintelligent. They show lack of interest, involvement, and motivation for academic success. They show general academic underachievement. The cumulative deficiencies in learning ultimately lead to their wastage and stagnation. These children are socially, economically, and educationally disadvantaged. School readiness programmes in preschool centres, enriched experiences, and remedial instruction are very useful for them.

5. Needs and Problems of Exceptional Children

All children have certain basic needs. The needs of children are often accompanied by or result in certain problems. The needs and problems of exceptional children are similar to and at the same time different from those of non-exceptional children. The needs and problems of exceptional children also vary depending upon the direction and degree of their deviation from normal children and their type of exceptionality. For example, the needs and problems of mildly and moderately handicapped children are different from those of severely handicapped children. Similarly the needs and problems of handicapped children are different from those of children with superior ability. Even though the needs and problems of exceptional children are related to their characteristics they have certain common needs and problems such as, need for appropriate education, need for independent functioning, need for respect for their individuality, etc.

Disabled children are like non-disabled children except their specific disabilities. For example, a blind child is like any other sighted child except his loss of vision. Disabled children have a fundamental right to live and participate fully in all settings and programmes that are as normalized as possible. But consciously or out of ignorance we tend to treat them differently in school, at home, in the work place, and in the community. Our differential treatment creates in them and among their peers a feeling of 'otherness'.

Disabled children have a strong desire for independent functioning. Instead of assisting them to maximize their independent functioning in normal environments we make them dependent on others. It is perhaps for this reason that many blind and orthopaedically handicapped children resort to begging. One of the objectives of special education is to teach the disabled children self-help skills, daily living skills, vocational skills, and to assist them to manage their own affairs independently during adulthood.

An exceptional child, whether he is handicapped or gifted, has an individuality of his own. He thinks, learns, acts and adapts in his own way. He has the capabilities to live a better life and to improve his functioning level in the community. Teachers need to have confidence on his capabilities and respect for his individuality. In schools exceptional children do not have the opportunity to express themselves fully. Their individuality is suppressed and at times punished by teachers.

Exceptional children need free and appropriate education to maximize their capabilities. Such education should not be provided to them out of sympathy or as a privilege granted to them. Education is a basic human right and this must be granted to them just as we provide free and compulsory education to non-exceptional children. India is under pressure from international agencies to make education a basic right of the child. But it is surprising that the bill making education a basic right of the child is in the cold storage of the MHRD.

Many exceptional children and their parents experience difficulties relating to appropriate education. Appropriate education for exceptional children can only be provided in regular schools. But most teachers are reluctant to admit handicapped children in the regular schools on the false impression that educating handicapped children in regular schools will adversely affect the education of non-handicapped children. In most cases the blind, deaf and MR children are refused admission in regular schools. The principle of "zero reject" stipulates that no handicapped child should be denied the opportunity to receive education in a school of his choice. Moreover there is no provision of appropriate education for gifted and creative children in our schools excepting providing the same type of education that are provided to average students. There are also no special schools for gifted, creative, emotionally disturbed and even the learning disabled children.

The handicapped children need equality of educational opportunity. The indicators of equal education opportunity for the handicapped have been spelt out by NCERT (1987) as follows :

(i) Equal access to educational institutions in common with others.

(ii) Access to special education institutions where needed.

(iii) Resource facilities to support educational programmes.

(iv) Equal access to curriculum.

(v) Curriculum adjustment to the needs arising out of a disability wherever needed.

(vi) Adaptive aids and equipment to ensure optimal access to curriculum.

(vii) Adjustment of instructional methods and materials to ensure optimal access to curriculum.

(viii) Adjustment of evaluation and examination procedures to offset handicapping effects of the disability.

(ix) Trained manpower for equal educational opportunity in general and special institutions.

(x) Educational administrator's response to the needs of the disabled children.

(xii) Commitment to education and rehabilitation of the disabled.

The POA (NPE, 1986) also stipulates the above mentioned measures for appropriate education of handicapped children. But handicapped children experience problems of access to and success in educational institutions. There are a limited number of general schools enrolling handicapped children along with normal children. Even these schools are not properly equipped with materials, and special education provided in such schools is not appropriate to the needs of handicapped children. The evaluation and examination procedures are not adjusted to the special needs of such children.

Exceptional children need special education and related services. This requires proper assessment and classification of exceptional children. The problem is that in most cases the assessment procedure is not objective and systematic. This is why many children with temporary learning problems are classified as mentally retarded or learning disabled. Moreover, what is the cut-off points between a mildly retarded and moderately retarded? With limited and incomplete understanding about these children we tend to classify them and label them as retarded, deaf, handicapped, crippled, disabled, etc. Labelling itself is not a healthy practice for a number of reasons :

(i) Labels usually focus on a child's negative aspects. Once a child is labelled we tend to think about the child only in terms of his inadequacies or defects.

(ii) Labels lead to low expectations from teachers, parents and others about what a child can do.

(iii) Once a child is labelled teachers tend to explain the child's poor performance only in terms of his disability and not in terms of instructional failure.

(iv) A labelled child may develop a poor self-concept.

(v) Labels may lead to rejection by the peers.

(vi) Labels create a sense of helplessness, inferiority and stigmatization.

Exceptional children need special aids, equipment and learning materials to profit from regular and special education programmes and to meet their special needs. The blind children need braille materials and other aids; the low vision children need large print materials and magnifying glasses; the deaf children need hearing aids, speech trainer, visual materials, etc.; the MR children need games and play materials and other concrete objects; the LD children need alternate learning materials, work books, etc.; and so on. Gifted children need advanced learning materials, encyclopaedia, etc. In most schools aids, equipment and learning materials are not available for exceptional children. As a result exceptional children are not able to maximize their capabilities. Discrepancy between what they are capable of doing and what they do gradually widens. This also causes a huge wastage of human resources.

Exceptional children, particularly the disabled ones, need incentives and financial assistance — conveyance allowances, allowances for purchase of learning materials, uniform dress, etc. The state Governments are not in a position to provide such assistance to disabled children. They simply depend on the assistance provided by the MHRD, Govt. of India. In most states the education of disabled children has been neglected due to withdrawal of assistance by the MHRD, Govt. of India. This is a recurring problem for most disabled children.

6. How are Exceptional Children to be Educated?

There are various types of exceptional children. Educational programmes should vary from one category to other categories of exceptional children. Education of each category of exceptional children will be discussed separately in later chapters of this book. In this section a general discussion on their identification, assessment, placement and education has been made.

Identification and assessment : Many exceptional children remain unidentified whether they are in the school or out of school. Consequently they are not able to maximize their potentialities. This calls for early identification of such children. Regular teachers should observe the behavioural characteristics of children suspected to be exceptional and refer them to specialists for medical and psychological assessments. In our country, particularly in rural areas, school authorities have been facing difficulties for medical and psychological assessment of exceptional children due to non-availability of specialists. In such cases teachers can conduct functional assessment which indicates what a child can do and what he cannot do (Refer to Functional Assessment Guide developed by the Department of Teacher Education, Special Education and Extension Services, NCERT, New Delhi). Functional assessment is not a substitute for medical and psychological assessment. In every case exceptional children should be subjected to medical and psychological assessment if intervention programme is to be effective.

Placement services : After medical and psychological assessment exceptional children should be placed in a suitable grade in a suitable educational institution. The degree of deviation of an exceptional child and the nature and range of his previous experiences usually determine his placement in an educational institution. So far as handicapped children are concerned the following placement programmes are followed in our country :

(i) Full time placement in regular class.

(ii) Part time placement in regular class with part time placement in special class.

(iii) Full time placement in special class.

(iv) Full time placement in special schools.

(v) Full time placement in residential schools.

Since we do not have special class and special school provision for gifted, creative, emotionally disturbed and socially disadvantaged children, they are usually educated in regular schools. However, various types of scholarships such as NRTS, NTS, Merit scholarships, etc. are available for bright students.

Emphasis on individuality : Exceptional children constitute a heterogenous group. There are various categories of exceptional children. Each category of exceptional children has unique characteristics. Again in each category there are various classes of children depending upon their degree of uniqueness. Education of exceptional children should match with their individual characteristics. In fact the individuality of each exceptional child should be the basis of all that we are doing and all that we want to do for his education.

Emphasis on learning : It is worth noting that children are required to learn in the way the teacher teaches. Since emphasis is being shifted at present from teaching to learning, teachers should teach in the way the child learns best. This emphasis on learning rather than teaching is rightly justified while planning any educational programme for exceptional children, whether they are disabled, disturbed, disadvantaged or gifted.

Special school setting : In our country a large number of special schools have been established for education of severely handicapped children, particularly the blind, the deaf and the mentally retarded children. In special schools severely handicapped children are educated by specially trained teachers with the help of special aids and equipment and a curriculum adapted to their needs. Excepting a few Government institutions, education in special schools is very expensive. Thus, many handicapped children are forced to be out of schools as their parents are not in a position to meet the expenses of their children's education in special schools.

Integrated setting : The recent trend in the education of disabled children is to educate them in common with non-disabled children in general schools. The National Policy of Education (1986) envisages that "wherever it is possible, education of children with locomotor handicap and other mild handicaps will be common with that of others. Special schools with hostels will be provided, as far as possible, at district headquarters, for severely handicapped children.... Voluntary efforts for education of the disabled will be encouraged in every possible way."

Provision of incentives : Government of India have made certain provisions of incentives for the education of disabled children. These include transport allowances, uniform allowances, purchase of books, escort allowances, attendance scholarships, etc. Disabled children should be guided to take advantage of such incentives. In addition to these, gifted and talented children should be also guided to take advantage of NRTS, NTS and other scholarships.

Preparatory classes : Disabled children should have some preparation before they receive formal education in a school. Such preparation can be made either in a special school or in ECEC centre, anganwadi, balwadi or preparatory classes in a primary school. For this purpose the teacher should conduct a screening test first, and then administer individual tests, interview parents and their disabled children to assess what the child knows and can do and what he does not know or what he cannot do. A blind child must receive mobility training, orientation training and training in daily living skills and braille writing. A learning disabled child must be trained to sit and be attentive. Many disabled children need preparation in pre-academic skills. Such preparation is very essential for successful progress in primary grades. But once a child has completed preparation in pre-academic skills, communication skills, daily living skills, mobility training and orientation training he should be encouraged to receive education in a general school in common with others.

In integrated settings disabled and non-disabled children are taught by the regular class teacher with support from the resource teacher, and instruction in the resource room in areas of their deficiences. "The objective should be to integrate the physically and mentally handicapped with the general community, to prepare them for normal growth, and enable them to face life with courage and confidence" (NPE, 1986).

Resource teacher support : Every school admitting exceptional children should have a resource teacher for every 8 to 10 exceptional children. The resource teacher may be a full time resource teacher or an itinerant resource teacher. He is the person to provide support services to exceptional children in the resource room. Since he is an expert in the methodology of educating exceptional children he can also act as a consultant to other regular teachers.

Aids and equipment : Exceptional children who do not profit from the conventional instructional materials, teaching aids and equipment should be provided with aids and equipment in the resource room keeping in view their special needs. Braille materials, large print materials and magnifying glasses for the visually impaired, hearing aids, speech trainer, and visual materials for the hearing impaired, play and toy materials for the mentally retarded, alternate learning materials for the less abled ones, etc. should be made available in schools for proper education of exceptional children.

2

Special Education

1. What is Special Education?

Special education means specially designed instruction which meets the special educational and related needs of an exceptional child. It is distinguished from regular educational programme meant for non-exceptional children by some unusual quality, something uncommon, noteworthy. It is something special — special materials, special training techniques, special equipment and special help and/or special facilities may be required for special categories of children having special needs. For example, visually impaired children may require reading materials in large print or braille. Hearing impaired children may require hearing aid, auditory training, lip reading etc. Orthopaedically handicapped children may require wheel chairs, and removal of architectural barriers. Mentally retarded children may need skill training. Related services, such as special transportation, medical and psychological assessment, physical and occupational therapy and counselling may be required if special education is to be effective.

Special education as teaching : We may look at special education in terms of *who*, *what*, *where*, and *how*. *Who*? Special education is meant for exceptional children whose special needs or abilities necessitate an individualized programme of education. An inter-disciplinary team of professionals — special educators, regular classroom teachers, psychologists, speech therapists, physiotherapists, specialist doctors bear the primary responsibility for helping exceptional children maximize their capabilities. *What* ? Special education is sometimes differentiated from regular education by its curriculum — that is, by what is taught. For example, teaching self-help skills or training in reading and writing braille is an important part of curriculum for severely handicapped children (the blind) in special education institutions which is not found in regular education. It is said that in regular education the school system dictates the curriculum, but in special education the child's individual needs dictate the curriculum. *Where*? Special education can sometimes be identified by where it takes place. Whereas regular education is provided in the regular classroom, special education may be provided in special class, resource room, special school or in residential school. *How*? Special education can be differentiated from regular education by the method used by teachers. One special educator may use sign language to communicate with his students. Another special educator may use task analysis and skill training for mentally retarded children. Still another special educator may use multisensory approach and process training while teaching a LD child.

Special education as intervention : Special education is an intervention strategy to eliminate, or at least reduce, the obstacles that might keep a child with disabilities from full and active participation in school and society. There are three basic kinds of intervention efforts such as :

— Preventive Efforts (Keeping possible problems from becoming a serious handicap).

— Remedial Programmes (Overcoming disability through training or education).

— Compensatory Efforts (Giving the child new ways to deal with the disability).

Special education is a profession, a service with tools and techniques to meet the special needs of exceptional children. It is individually planned, systematically implemented, and carefully evaluated instruction to help exceptional learners achieve the greatest possible personal self-sufficiency and success in present and future environments (Heward and Orlansky, 1992).

2. Principles of Special Education

Special education is based on the following principles :

Individual differences : There are inter-individual differences and intra-individual differences. In other words, some students are very different from most in ways that are specific regarding education, and special education is required to meet their educational needs.

Zero reject : All children with disabilities must be provided a free and appropriate education. The school systems do not have the option to accept or reject a child for education in a regular school.

Non-discriminatory evaluation : Students who need special education must be clearly identified to ensure that they receive appropriate services. Each student must receive a full individual examination before being placed in a special education programme with tests appropriate to his cultural and linguistic background. A re-evaluation is required at intervals to assess his progress and difficulties in learning.

Individualized education programme : Students with special needs require individualized education programme either in a resource room or a special class in the regular school for some part of the day. Such education must match with their current level of functioning and their special needs.

Least restrictive environment : As much as possible, children with handicaps must be educated with children who are not handicapped in the regular classroom. The regular classroom provides the least restrictive environment for handicapped children.

Due process : Due process implies that the parents of handicapped children have the right to evaluate the efforts of the school system to identify and assess the handicapped children, to modify the programme of the school to meet the special needs of these children and, if they are not satisfied with the programme of the school, they have the right to withdraw their children from that school for a better programme in any other educational institution.

Parental participation : Special education can be made effective if parents participate actively in the educational programme designed for handicapped children.

3. History of Special Education

There have always been exceptional children, but there have not always been special educational services to meet their needs. The historical roots of special education are found in Europe and America primarily in the 19th century. In ancient civilization handicapped children were either killed or subject to abuse and neglect. Prior to the 19th century there were isolated instances of acceptance, kindly care, and education of disabled children.

Systematic efforts to provide special education to handicapped children started in the 19th century in Europe and America. Most of the originators of special education were European physicians. But the Americans who were initially concerned with the care and training of the handicapped kept themselves informed about the development that took place in Europe. Even some Americans used to visit Europe to get first-hand knowledge about the education of handicapped children. It is a fact that European physicians were initially concerned about the education of mentally retarded children. Similarly much of the initial work in the field of special education in America centered around deaf and blind children.

The history of special education does not indicate "Europe, good — America bad". But it is true that important ideas in special education found their way from Europe to America. Many European and American physicians and educators contributed greatly to the development of special education, most prominent among them were :

J.M.G. Itard,	Samuel Gridley Howe,
E. Seguin,	T.H. Gallaudet,
Sigmund Freud,	Philipe Pinel,
Anne Sullivan.	

Development of special education in Europe : Itard's contribution. Itard, a French physician, is the person to whom most historians trace the beginning of special education. In the beginning years of 19th century, Itard set about to educate a wild boy of 11 or 12, named Victor. The boy was apparently abandoned in a forest in Southern France at the age of 3 or 4. He managed to survive until his capture. At the time of capture he was animal like in appearance and behaviour. He was naked, dirty, scarred, and unable to speak, and he selected food by smell. Itard could not make him normal, but he did dramatically improve his behaviour through patient and systematic educative procedure.

Itard was the originator of instructional devices, the inventor of behaviour modification techniques, the first speech specialist, creator of oral education of the deaf, and father of special education for the mentally retarded and the physically handicapped. His work with Victor firmly established that the retarded could learn and improve.

Seguin's Contribution : Seguin is known as the greatest teacher of the mentally deficient. Being influenced by the achievements of Itard he established the first public school for the feeble-minded in Paris in 1837. In 1846 he published his classic textbook *Idiocy and Its Treatment by the Physiological Method.* His concept of education was the promotion of the harmonious physical, intellectual, and moral developments of the child. His techniques and materials later became the basis for the so-called Montessori Method. Seguin migrated to America and worked in collaboration with Samuel Howe for the education of mentally retarded.

The sensational discoveries and revolutionary ideas of Itard, Seguin and their successors during the 19th century which have formed the foundation for present day special education are as follows :

(i) Individualised instruction for the mentally retarded.

(ii) A carefully sequenced series of educational tasks for the mentally retarded.

(iii) Emphasis on stimulation.

(iv) Meticulous arrangement of the child's environment.

(v) Immediate reward for correct performance.

(vi) Tutoring in functional skills.

(vii) A belief that everyone should be educated to the greatest extent possible.

(viii) An assumption that every child can improve to some degree.

Development of special education in America : It is true that much of the initial work in the development of special education took place in Europe. But there were many Americans who contributed greatly during those early years.

Louis Braille's contributions : Louis Braille was the most important figure in the history of education of the blind. Braille, who became blind due to an accident during his early childhood, developed a revolutionary system of reading and writing for the blind. The Braille method is still recognised as the most appropriate method of reading and writing for the blind.

Howe's contribution : Samuel Gridly Howe was one of the first physicians in the United States to develop keen interest in the education of blind and deaf children. His phenomenal success with one of his pupils, Laura Bridgmen, a deaf-blind-mute, earned him international fame.

Anne Sullivan's contribution : Sullivan was a student of Howe. She was greatly influenced by her teacher's training methods. Although she was visually handicapped, she served as Helen Keller's tutor. Helen Keller was deaf-blind-mute. Sullivan's dedicated efforts could bring astonishing results. Helen quickly learned the names of objects and events in her environment. By the age of ten, she learned to say aloud "I — am — not — dumb — now". Later she became a graduate and wrote a number of books.

Gallaudet's contribution : Thomas Hopkins Gallaudet had keen interest in the education of the deaf. He established the first American residential school for the deaf in 1817 in Hartford. The Gallaudet College in Washington D.C., which is the only college for the deaf was named in his honour.

The fall and rise of special education : There were many other European and American physicians and educators whose fascinating and brilliant careers helped to shape special education. In fact, the early years of special education were vibrant with the pulse of new ideas of great physicians and educators. The results they achieved with handicapped children were truly remarkable. But despite the energy, optimism, and achievements of these early leaders, special education lost its momentum during the last part of the 19th century. Pessimism took hold, humane and effective treatment turned to ineffective institutionalization and human warehousing, hope turned to despair. The special schools which were opened in the late 1800s became dumping grounds for all kinds of misfits. Many factors were responsible for the decline of special education such as :

(i) Too much expectations of parents for their disabled children to achieve miraculous cure too soon.

(ii) Total failure of special education personnel in some cases.

(iii) Disagreement among professionals about the appropriate method of education.

(iv) Lack of financial support for providing special education services to a large number of disabled children.

(v) Social, political, and economic turmoil resulting from the civil war.

(vi) The idea that the handicapped were inherently inferior and not amenable to improvement through education.

(vii) The influence of Charles Darwin's theory of evolution — the survival of the fittest.

After the World War II special education made a come back with wealthy and powerful people like President Kennedy and President Johnson taking interest in the education of all the handicapped. Education of the handicapped was initially considered as a privilege. With the development of democracy and socialism in different countries of the world education was considered to be a basic right of the child. This realization paved the way for mainstreaming disabled children.

Influence of other disciplines : Special education did not suddenly spring up as a new discipline, nor did it develop in isolation from other disciplines. In the 20th century, members of the medical profession has continued to play important roles in the field of special education. The emergence of the disciplines of psychology and sociology and the widespread use of mental tests in the early years of the 20th century had enormous implications for the growth of the special education profession. Psychologists' study of learning and their prediction of success or failure in school learning helped focus attention on children with special educational needs. Sociologists and social workers drew attention to the ways in which the family and the community affect exceptional child's learning and development.

Contemporary special education draws heavily on all disciplines concerned with child development — medicine, psychology, sociology and social work. Special education, which was initially the concern of physicians and later of psychologists, is growing very fast to become an independent discipline. Opening up of M.A. (Special education), M.Ed. (Special Education) and B.Ed. (Special Education) in different University Departments and Colleges is an indication of this trend.

Development of special education in India : Special Education in India has a short history. There is no verifiable record of special education for exceptional children in ancient India or thereafter during the pre-independence period excepting few special schools for the blind which were established during the last part of the 19th century. After independence, the Constitution of India was framed in 1950. In pursuance of the provision made in Article 45 of the Constitution measures were taken to provide free, compulsory and universal primary education to all children in the age group of 6 to 14 including the handicapped children. Few special schools were opened in different States for blind and deaf children during the period 1950-1970. The number of special schools for blind, deaf and M.R. children established by Government increased thereafter. These schools catered to the needs of severely handicapped children. Training centres for teachers of handicapped children were also established by the Central Government and State Governments. But mildly and moderately handicapped children were deprived of special education facilities. Three situations were noticed with regard to education of mildly and moderately handicapped children in our country :

(i) Most of them were out of school;

(ii) Some of them were forced to receive education in special schools and

(iii) Some of them remained unidentified and uncared for in general schools leading to their wastage and stagnation.

After 1974 attempts were made to educate mildly and moderately handicapped children in general schools having IED units.

The dismal picture of the education of handicapped children in our country continued up to the formulation of National Policy of Education (1986). The NPE (1986) put emphasis on mainstreaming the handicapped children with the general community. It states : "The objective should be to integrate the physically and mentally handicapped with the general community as equal partners, to prepare them for normal growth and to enable them to face life with courage and confidence." This resulted in modification of our attitude towards the disabled, new realization about the educability of the disabled, establishment of new special schools for the blind, deaf and severely mentally retarded, higher enrolment of mildly and moderately handicapped children in general schools, appointment and training of resource teachers, etc.

The Project Integrated Education for the Disabled (PIED) was implemented in different blocks, and the Centrally Sponsored Scheme of IED was also seriously implemented in different States to create awareness, organise parent contact programme and community contact programme, provide training to regular teachers on IED and to monitor and evaluate the system of IED. Voluntary agencies and NGOs came forward in large numbers to cater to the special educational and related needs of disabled children.

Special education in India has become so popular that different Universities have already started new courses — B.Ed. (Special Education) and M.Ed. (Special Education). Even research scholars have also come forward to undertake research projects leading to Ph.D. (Special Education). As new research findings are established, the scope of special education has widened and the concept of disabled children has also undergone a change. Now disabled children are regarded as "Children with Special Needs" and as "Differently Abled Children".

During the short period of 1950 to the end of the 20th century, special education has developed so much that it deserves to be considered as an independent discipline.

4. Objectives of Special Education

Special education has the same objectives as those of regular education — human resource development through providing appropriate education to children, national development, social reconstruction, civic development, vocational efficiency, etc. In addition to these objectives special education has certain special objectives such as the following :

(i) Early identification and assessment of special needs of handicapped children.

(ii) Early intervention to prevent a handicapping condition from becoming a serious one for remediation of learning problems and compensation by teaching the child new ways of doing things.

(iii) Parent counselling about prevention and remediation of defects, care, and training of handicapped children in daily living skills, self-help skills, pre-academic skills and communication skills.

(iv) Community mobilization and awareness of problems of handicapped children and their education.

(v) Rehabilitation of the handicapped.

The National Policy of Education (1986/1992) clearly stipulates that :

"The objective should be (i) to integrate the physically and mentally handicapped with the general community as equal partners, (ii) to prepare them for normal growth and (iii) to enable them to face life with courage and confidence."

The following measures have been envisaged in the Programme of Action (NPE — 1986) for attainment of these objectives :

(i) Wherever it is feasible, the education of children with motor handicaps and other mild handicaps will be common with that of others.

(ii) Special schools with hostels will be provided, as far as possible, at district headquarters, for severely handicapped children.

(iii) Adequate arrangements will be made to give vocational training to the disabled.

(iv) Teacher training programmes will be reoriented in particular for teachers of primary classes to deal with special difficulties of handicapped children.

(v) Voluntary efforts for education of the disabled will be encouraged in every possible way.

5. The Resource Teacher

Who is a Resource Teacher? : The resource teacher is a key person in the IED programme. The success or failure of the IED programme depends primarily upon how the resource person implements the programme. He is the specialist teacher, special education teacher, or the support teacher who provides the support services to the disabled children studying in the IED school. But he is not an extra teacher in the school as he is sometimes considered by the regular teachers of the school.

Appointment of Resource Teacher : The centrally sponsored scheme of IED has provision for appointment of one resource teacher for every 8 disabled children enrolled in the Primary or Secondary school. If a particular school does not have 8 disabled children on roll then one resource teacher can be appointed for a cluster of schools in a particular locality. Such a teacher who is called an itinerant teacher has to visit a number of schools implementing the scheme of IED and attend to the special needs of disabled children studying in these schools. Resource teachers are to be appointed by the competent authority empowered by the government following the normal recruitment procedure.

Qualification : The minimum qualification for the post of resource teacher as envisaged in the centrally sponsored scheme of IED is :

(i) 10+2 with D.Ed. (Special Education) for Primary stage and

(ii) B.A. or B.Sc. with B.Ed. (Special Education) for secondary stage.

The candidates must have D.Ed./B.Ed. (Special Education) with specialisation in any field such as visual impairment, hearing impairment, mental retardation, etc.

Scale of pay : The resource teacher gets the same scale of pay as applicable to other regular teachers in the respective category.

Special pay : The resource teachers are entitled to a special pay of Rs. 150 p.m. in urban areas and Rs. 200 p.m. in rural areas in addition to their pay.

Training/Preparation : The resource teachers are required to prepare themselves adequately and develop their competencies so that they can perform their functions successfully. A resource teacher has to attend training programmes, short orientation courses, and refresher courses organised by various agencies from time to time. The following courses are offered by various institutes :

D.Ed. (Deaf)	—	Regional Training Centres for Teachers of the Deaf, National Institutes for Hearing Handicap.
B.Ed. (Deaf)	—	National Institutes for Hearing Handicap.
D.Ed. (Blind)	—	Regional Training Centres for Teachers of the Blind, National Institutes for Visual Handicap.
Diploma in M.R.	—	National Institutes for Mental Retardation, Chetana Institute of Mental Retardation.
Short-Orientation Courses & Refresher Courses	—	State Council of Educational Research and Training, Regional Institutes of Education, National Council of Educational Research and Training.

Duties and Responsibilities of a Resource Teacher : The resource teacher is a catalyst who works for the successful implementation of the scheme of IED. He is like a mirror to reflect the policy of the government for the welfare of handicapped children. He has a number of duties and responsibilities. He has to work very closely with handicapped children in collaboration with other regular teachers, community members, parents, specialists and administrative personnel. His duties and responsibilities can be discussed under three heads :

(a) Before the school hour

(b) During the school hour

(c) After the school hour

(a) Before the School Hour

(i) *Identification of disabled children* : The resource teacher has to conduct community survey and, if possible, door to door survey to identify disabled children in different categories in different age groups, sex wise, and in-school and out-of-school.

(ii) *Creating awareness* : The resource teacher has to create awareness among community members, parents and teachers about education of disabled children in general schools. Such awareness can be created through community contact programme, parent contact programmes, and in centre-meetings of primary school teachers. The resource teacher can make use of video cassettes and seek the assistance of health personnel and other experts for the above purpose.

(iii) *Arranging preparatory classes* : In most cases the resource teacher may find that disabled children seeking admission in the general school have not learnt certain skills which are prerequisite to learning academic skills in the school. In such cases, instead of admitting the children directly in Class-I the resource teacher has to prepare them for a period of one to two years in prerequisite skills. He has, therefore, to arrange preparatory classes (Prep-I and Prep-II) for those disabled children who are in need of it.

(iv) *Assessment of disabled children* : One primary responsibility of the resource teacher is to arrange for medical and psychological assessment of disabled children. If such assessment is not possible due to unavailability of the assessment team or other reasons he has to conduct functional assessment before he starts formal training.

(b) During the School Hour

(i) *Care of disabled children* : During the school hour the resource teacher is in full charge of disabled children. Like any other teacher, the resource teacher has to play the role of a mother in taking care of disabled children. He should be "at their service" any time.

(ii) *Full and special attention* : The resource teacher has to pay full and special attention to disabled children to meet their special needs.

(iii) *Periodical testing* : The resource teacher is expected to conduct periodical testing for disabled children. He should first conduct a screening test for all disabled children at the time of enrollment. Then he should administer individual test on those children who failed in the screening test. This will given him a clear picture about the abilities and specific limitations of disabled children and how he should proceed in teaching them.

(iv) *Maintaining pupil information card* : The resource teacher has to maintain a 'Pupil Information Card' for each and every disabled child. Such a card which is made up-to-date from time to time should contain bio-data, family background, what the child can do, what he cannot do, his problems and difficulties, intervention required, etc.

(v) *A referral agent* : The resource teacher has to act as a referral agent. He is the right person to understand the disabled child better. Whenever he notices any specific problem with the child which is beyond his ability to deal with he may refer the case to appropriate specialist for intervention.

(vi) *Maintaining the resource room* : The resource teacher has to maintain the resource room with all the aids, equipment and materials which are required for specialised instruction.

(vii) *Resource room teaching* : The primary duty of a resource teacher is teaching the disabled children in the resource room. Lip reading, daily living skills, social skills, communication skills, academic skills and remedial teaching are fundamental aspects of resource room teaching. The amount of time required for resource room teaching for disabled children depends upon the degree of their disability and the nature and type of home training received by such children prior to their enrollment in the school.

(viii) *Regular classroom teaching* : In addition to teaching disabled children the resource teacher should also teach in regular classrooms. The resource teacher is not a subject teacher, but a specialist in the methodology of IED. His teaching to disabled and non-disabled children in the regular classroom will enable him to understand how non-disabled children accept their disabled peers, and how the disabled children are able to adjust with their non-disabled peers, and other regular teachers.

(ix) *Positive attitude towards the disabled* : Equally important for the resource teacher is the fact the he should show positive attitude towards disabled children. He should avoid as far as possible and advice other regular teachers to avoid labeling of any kind because labeling has adverse effect on the child's personality and ego development. In order to develop in the child a positive ego/self-concept the resource teacher should provide success experience to him. A child may be disabled in some respect but he may have potentiality for success in other areas. This is why disabled children are now called 'differently able' children. The teacher should recognise his potentialities for success and arrange activities and provide opportunities to the child to succeed.

(x) *Organising cocurricular activities* : Related to the above is the duty of a resource teacher to organise cocurricular activities such as sports and athletic events, music, dance and drama, drawing and painting exhibition, etc. The resource teacher must ensure that both disabled and non-disabled students participate cooperatively and competitively in such activities. Such activities like the Special Olympics have tremendous value in knowing each other, identifying the talents, harnessing and improving their talents, positive ego development, mutual respect and acceptance among disabled and non-disabled children.

(xi) *Consultant for regular teachers* : The resource teacher has to act as a consultant to other regular teachers. He should help and advice regular teachers in the methodology of teaching, making seat arrangement, and in all matters relating to mainstreaming of disabled children.

(xii) *A link* : The resource teacher should act as a link between regular teachers and disabled students, administrators and the school parents and teachers.

(xiii) *Help and advice in rehabilitation* : The resource teacher should also provide help and advise disabled children and their parents in rehabilitation, vocational training and further education of such children.

(c) After the School Hour

(i) *Counselling to parents.* The resource teacher should give counselling to parents on the care of the mother during pregnancy, pre-natal and post-natal care, care of the eye and ear, language and other training at home, services available in various centres, etc. Parent contact programme and home visits give opportunity to the resource teacher for the above purpose.

(ii) *Arranging resources* : The resource teacher's responsibilities are not limited to teaching the disabled children with the available resources in the school. He should try to arrange resources for the IED unit from various service agencies and Departments of government such as the Rotary Club, Lion's Club, Social Welfare, Child Welfare, Vocational Rehabilitation Centre, UNICEF, NCERT, SCERT, business organisation and community leaders.

6. The Resource Room

What is a Resource Room? : The resource room is a fast growing and a very common educational arrangement for disabled children studying in general schools. It is essentially a special setting in a school to which disabled children can be referred for brief periods of specialised instruction which they might not be able to receive in the regular classroom. In short it is a place where disabled children get the assistance from the specialist teacher. The resource room is not "any room" of the school because a room should have some important provisions to enable it to the name 'resource'. But it is possible to convert 'any room' into a resource room and exploit the best of the available facilities. For this purpose improvisation is necessary. The Centrally Sponsored Scheme of Integrated Education for disabled children visualises, "The resource room may be set up preferably in an existing room in the school. A new room may be built only where no accommodation is available to the satisfaction of the state Government. Grant shall be available for construction of resource room in schools in such circumstances subject to a maximum of Rs. 40,000". If this grant is inadequate the Village Education Committee or the School Managing Committee may be involved to bear the additional expenditure to be incurred in the construction of the resource room.

Resource Room, Special Class, and Resource Centre : The three terms mentioned above need little explanation to avoid confusion. If a disabled child is enrolled in a class with specially trained teacher, and spends most of the day there, it is usually referred to as a special class. If, on the other hand, the disabled child is enrolled in the regular classroom and goes to the special room only for specialised instruction for brief periods of time, say 1 or 2 periods every day it is usually called a resource room. Thus, the difference between a special class and a resource room depends upon the amount of time spent by the disabled child in the special room. Ideally speaking every primary school implementing the scheme of IED should have resource room facilities. A resource centre, on the other hand, is properly equipped with staff and material which can be shared by a number of schools in a particular locality. For all practical purposes a special school can serve as a resource centre for all IED schools in the locality. There should be three types of resource centres such as :

(i) The State Resource Centre to be set up in the State capital or in the institution which coordinates the implementation of the scheme of IED in the state.

(ii) The District Resource Centre to be set up in each district headquarters, and

(iii) The Block Resource Centre to be set up in each block headquarters.

How a Resource Room should be like?

(i) A resource room is not a formal classroom where abled and disabled children attend formal lessons from the first period till the last period.

(ii) It does not belong to a particular child or class. All disabled children in different categories and studying in different classes should be given resource room facilities. All disabled children studying in the school should have access to it.

(iii) It should be centrally located in the school so that disabled children can reach the room without any difficulty and without wasting time and energy to reach the room. If it is located in a corner of the school the disabled children may waste unnecessarily much time and energy to reach the room.

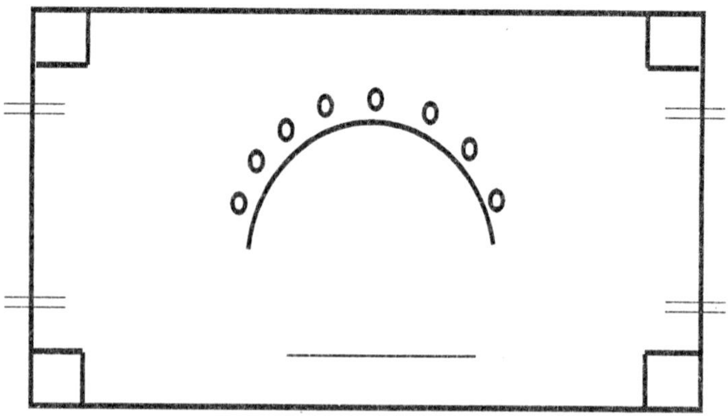

Fig. 1 Resource Room

(iv) It should be properly electrified to facilitate use of aids and instruments which are required for their specialised training.

(v) The resource room should have good lighting condition and furniture. This will give a psychological comfort to the disabled children.

(vi) The resource room should not be a big one. The size of the resource room should be 15" x 10" which is sufficient to accommodate 4 to 8 disabled children at a given time.

(vii) The resource room should be free from unnecessary noises. Children should not be assembled in the resource room unless they have specific work to do.

(viii) The resource room should have equipment and materials which are required for specialised instruction and training. What type of equipment and materials are to be stored in the resource room? Equipment and materials vary from programme to programme (programme for visually impaired, programme for hearing impaired, programme for mentally retarded and so on). Equipment will also vary according to the level of the programme (primary, secondary of preschool education or preparatory classes). Equipment will also vary according to use (use by individual children, use by a group of children, and sharing amongst schools.) Thus, it is not possible to make a list of all the equipment and materials required for every resource room. However, a list of aids and equipment required for disabled children category-wise and according to use is given in the next section of this chapter.

Need/Importance of Resource Room

A resource room is needed for the following reasons :

(i) *Additional help* : The disabled children need additional help or support services from the resource teacher to cope with non-disabled children.

(ii) *Specialised instruction* : The disabled children need equal educational experiences to learn the academic skills. Equal educational experiences necessiate specialised instruction in difficult areas. Specialised instruction can only be given in the special room. The resource room is also necessary for providing remedial instruction, assignments and enrichment reading etc.

(iii) *Functional assessment* : The disabled children are to be assessed properly before formal instruction is started. But in most cases specialists are not available, particularly in rural areas, to conduct medical and psychological assessment.

The resource teacher can conduct functional assessment which will indicate what the child can do, what he can not do, his educational needs, etc. Functional assessment is to be conducted with the help of toys and play materials and in a conducive environment. The resource room is the place which provides a conducive environment for carrying on functional assessment of disabled children.

(iv) *Privacy* : The resource teacher is required to interview the parents and their disabled children for purpose of gathering information about the problems, difficulties and special needs of such children. This calls for privacy to be ensured. The special room provides the privacy which is basic to understanding disabled children and their needs.

(v) *Individual attention* : The disabled children have certain special needs. This also necessiates individual attention to disabled children. The resource teacher can pay individual attention to disabled children in a special room only.

(vi) *Preparing instructional materials* : The resource teacher is required to prepare instructional materials which may be necessary for specialised instruction. He has also to display the materials in a special room. He needs space for storing the materials and using different aids and appliances during specialised instruction. A special room is needed for preparation, storing, display and use of aids and equipment. A well maintained resource room also gives a general idea to the visitors about the type of services provided to disabled children.

7. Aids and Equipment

Importance of Aids and Equipment : The success or failure of integrated education for the disabled depends critically upon the availability of aids and equipment for learning purposes. The importance of aids and equipment in the education of disabled children can be stated as follows :

(i) If a teacher can present concepts, ideas or principles through spoken words, it is fine. But disabled children in general, and mentally retarded, learning disabled and the hearing impaired children in particular, do not learn as much as they are capable of learning through teacher's verbalisation. Aids and equipment help the teacher to avoid excessive, empty and meaningless verbalisation in teaching.

(ii) Specially designed teaching aids provide direct sense experience to the disabled.

(iii) They help disabled children to form clear and accurate concepts in different subjects.

(iv) They help teachers in communication of ideas in a more effective way.

(v) They provide concrete and specific experiences to the disabled children.

(vi) Teaching aids and equipment are not substitutes for teacher's presentation. Rather they supplement ideas gained through other means.

(vii) They help in creating and sustaining children's interest in learning situation.

(viii) They make disabled learners active and enthusiastic in learning different subjects.

(ix) They help in effective teaching, efficient learning and consequently in better retention.

(x) Aids and equipment add colour and beauty to the resource room. A resource room without aids and equipment is like a deserted river.

Although teaching aids and equipment are valuable means of teaching and learning, they should not be used indiscriminately for all disabled children and in all situations by all teachers. Moreover some of the aids and equipment are very costly. In such cases equipment available in one school should be shared by a number of schools in the locality. For example, brailler and speech trainers cannot be supplied to or purchased by every primary school. These equipment can be shared by five to ten schools in the locality. Whether teaching aids are supplied free of cost to the schools or the schools have to arrange their own aids it is always desirable to have improvised, low-cost or no-cost aids.

Aids and equipment required for a resource room. What are the specific aids and equipment necessary for a resource room? It is a question which has no precise answer because :

(i) Aids and equipment vary from programme to programme. For example, if the school implements a programme for visually impaired children, the aids and equipment will be different from those required for a school which implements a programme for hearing impaired children. Similarly teaching aids meant for mentally retarded children or learning disabled children are different from those meant for hearing impaired children.

Requirements of Equipment for Resource Room Disability-wise : Inventory of Equipment and Materials

Disability	Aids and Equipment			
	Individual Use	Sharing within school	Sharing amongst schools	Institional material
Orthopaedic	Adjustable furniture, special writing material, thick pen.	Adjustable furniture, Provision for development of improvised prosthetics.	—	—
Visually Impaired Blind	Braille slate and Stylus, Abacus, Taylor frame, Mobility canes.	Brailler, Abacus, Taylor frame, Cassette and talking books, Maps, Recreational material, Embossed recreational materials.	Braille sheets, Thermoform machine, Indu Brailler Maintenance services for Brailler, Embossed recreational materials.	Braille Text-books, Matrial on cassette and talking books.
Partially sighted and Low vision children	Special adaptive equipment like hand magnifiers to be used with spectacles, portable reading lamps.	Specially designed desks with adjustable magnifiers, white boards in place of black boards.	Special arrangements for producing large print materials.	Large print materials.

Hearing Impaired	Individual hearing aids.	Voice trainer, Mirror in size of 3' x 6' for speech therapy, big mirrors 10' x 6' in each classroom, Group hearing aids, cells for hearing aids. Picture albums.	Audiometer, Voice trainer, Maintenance facilities for hearing aids.	Special learning materials like flash cards, charts, educational games, handouts of classroom activities.
Mentally Retarded	Play materials Toys	Sensory apparatus and kits prepared on the lines of Maria Montessori kits or produced by NCERT for Early Childhood Care and Education.		Material written on a lower reading level than average.

(ii) Teaching aids will vary according to the level of the programme—elementary education or secondary education.

(iii) Aids and equipment also vary according to their use. Some aids and equipment are meant for use by individual children (*e.g.*, individual hearing aid). Some aids are meant for sharing within the school or use by a group of children at the same time (*e.g.*, group hearing aids, maps, charts, pictures, etc.). Some aids and equipment can be shared amongst schools in a particular locality (*e.g.* speech trainer, brailler, etc.)

Thus, it is not possible to prepare a list of aids and equipment required for a resource room. However, an inventory of aids and equipment required for various categories of disabled children and according to their use is given at pages 36 and 37. Specific teaching aids for learning disabled children have not been indicated in this table. Because learning disabled children need the same teaching aids which are required for (effective) teaching normal children.

8. Types of Special Education Services

The type of special education services available for disabled children can be structured along a continuum that ranges from integration to segregation or full-time placement of disabled children in the regular classroom to twenty four-hour institutional care. The type of services required depends primarily on the degree of disability and the nature of special needs. Seriously and profoundly handicapped children usually require more continuous, prolonged, and intensive care in special institutions. The following are various services available for handicapped children.

(i) *Full-time placement in a regular classroom* : The least intensive level of special education service is placement of the disabled child in a regular classroom. The regular classroom teacher is provided with materials, equipment and instructional methods that are appropriate to the disabled child. At this level, the direct services of experts may not be required. The expertise of the regular classroom teacher may be sufficient to meet the child's needs. Usually speech handicapped, mildly mentally retarded, learning disabled, orthopaedically handicapped, visually impaired children who can work independently with braille materials and the hard-of-hearing children can be full-time students in regular classroom.

(ii) *Full-time placement in a regular classroom with special education consultations* : At the next level, the disabled child is a full time student in a regular classroom. The regular teacher has special materials and equipment to teach the disabled child. But he may need consultation with the special educator. The special educator instructs the regular teacher for selection and use of special materials, equipment and methods.

(iii) *Full-time placement in a regular classroom with provision of itinerant special educator service* : Going a step further, the disabled child is a full-time student in a regular classroom. But he gets the services of an itinerant teacher. The itinerant teacher moves from school to school on a planned schedule and works directly with disabled children either individually or in small groups. He provides specialised instruction to the disabled child once or twice in a week and advises the regular teacher in the use of materials, equipment and methods. This plan can be used in rural areas where schools are far apart and too small to have full-time resource teachers.

(iv) *Full-time placement in a regular classroom with provision of a resource room/resource teacher* : At the next level, the disabled child is enrolled in the regular classroom. But he receives specialised instruction from a resource teacher in the resource room. The length and frequency of such help depend on the severity of his problems. The resource teacher provides such instruction in the special classroom. The child returns to the regular classroom and participates in regular classroom activities in music, art and physical education in the second half of the day.

(v) *Part-time placement in regular classroom with part-time placement in a special class* : In this type of service the disabled child is a member of a special classroom. In view of his moderate disability and special needs he receives specialised instruction in academic subjects in a special classroom of the school for a half-day. The resource teacher provides such instruction in the special classroom. The child returns to the regular classroom and participates in regular classroom activities in music, art and physical education in the second half of the day.

(vi) *Full-time placement in a special class* : This is the type of service usually provided to severely retarded children. This is also the oldest and traditional type of service for disabled children which has been criticised for it segregates disabled children from their normal peers. In this plan a group of ten to fifteen disabled children belonging to one particular category of disability are enrolled in a special class. Thus all MR children attend one special class. All hearing impaired children attend one special class. These children spend the whole day with the resource teacher in the special classroom being segregated from their normal peers in the school, except during recess, lunch, after school activities and school functions. In rural areas, where ten to

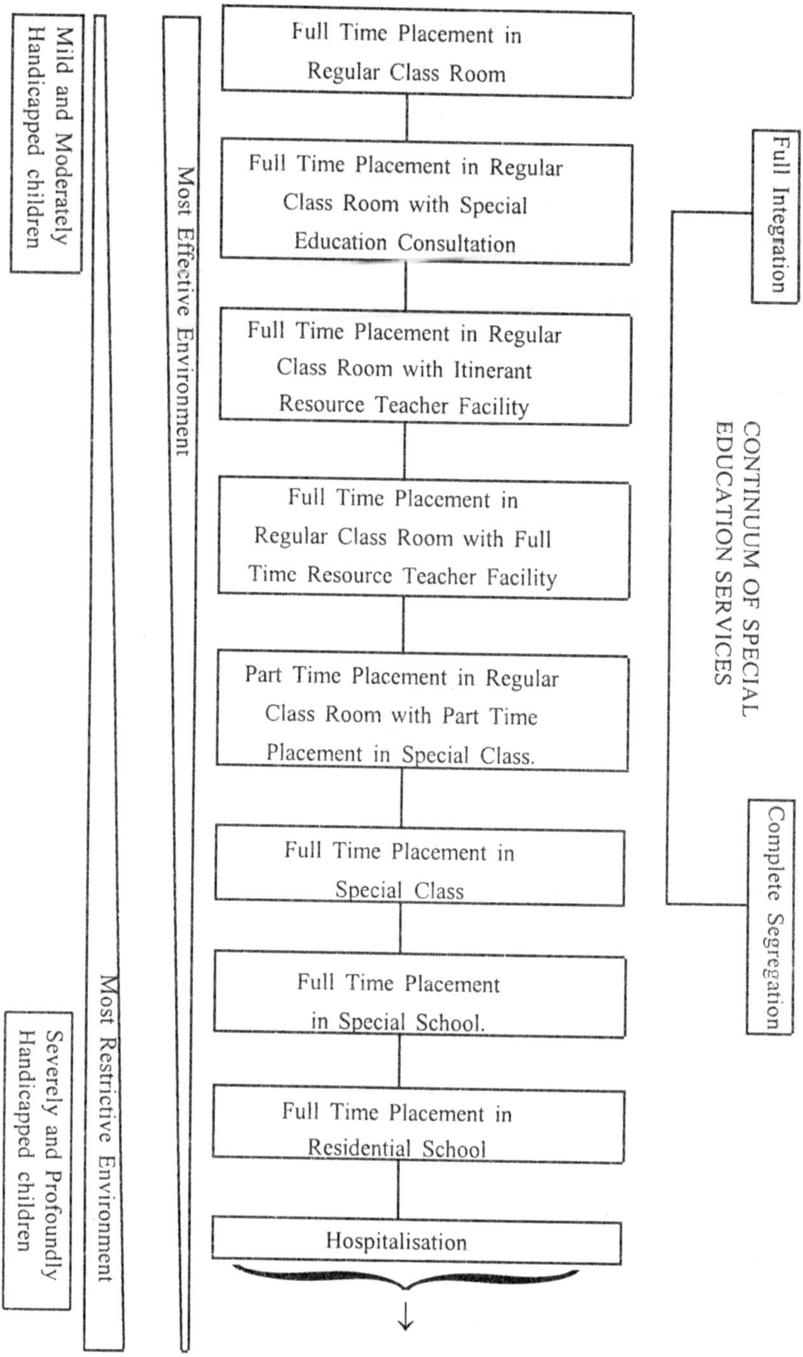
Mild and Moderately Handicapped children
Most Effective Environment
Full Time Placement in Regular Class Room
Full Time Placement in Regular Class Room with Special Education Consultation
Full Time Placement in Regular Class Room with Itinerant Resource Teacher Facility
Full Time Placement in Regular Class Room with Full Time Resource Teacher Facility
Part Time Placement in Regular Class Room with Part Time Placement in Special Class.
Full Time Placement in Special Class
Full Time Placement in Special School.
Full Time Placement in Residential School
Hospitalisation
Full Integration
CONTINUUM OF SPECIAL EDUCATION SERVICES
Complete Segregation
Severely and Profoundly Handicapped children
Most Restrictive Environment

fifteen children having same type of handicap are not available, children having different types of disability may be enrolled in a special class. But considerable demands are made on a teacher working with children with diverse problems.

(vii) *Full-time placement in special schools* : Special schools provide an all day, segregated experience for disabled children. The special school is usually organised for a specific category of disabled children. It contains special equipment necessary for their care and education. The children return to their home after the school hour. There are special schools for blind, deaf and mentally retarded children in our country.

(viii) *Full-time placement in a residential school* : The most restrictive type of services are usually provided in boarding or residential schools. This type of service is usually provided to blind, totally deaf, and profoundly retarded children. In this arrangement disabled children receive twenty four hour care in the boarding school. They are isolated from their parents, siblings and the community. But they can visit their homes during vacation and on weekends. In residential schools children receive academic instruction in addition to training in social skills, communication skills, self-help skills, etc.

(ix) *Hospital and home-bound instruction* : This involves teaching the handicapped children in the hospital or at home because of their physical and/or psychological conditions. This type of service is most often required for physically handicapped or emotionally disturbed children when no alternative is readily available. Typically, the child is confined to the hospital or his home for a relatively short period of time and the hospital or home-bound teacher maintains contact with the child's regular teacher.

Special education services in the past were much more restrictive and much less effective than they are today. Now placement of mildly and some moderately handicapped children in the least restrictive and most effective environment of the regular classroom is becoming increasingly common.

3

Integrated Education and Mainstreaming

1. Background

The education of disabled children never received such amount of consideration and special efforts by government and non-government agencies in past as in present days. The attitude of the community in general and the attitude of parents in particular towards the education of the disabled have undergone change with the development of society and civilisation. In the first phase, disabled children were treated with hostility and were neglected. They were considered as 'Curve of God' and a burden for the parents. They were often killed by their parents. In the second phase the disabled children were kept in protection and wardship. Mankind was subjected to a myth that "the disabled are useless, incapable of doing anything on their own, a species to be pitied and looked after as long as they are alive." Thus, no attempt was made for their education, training, habilitation, and rehabilitation. In the next phase, an attempt was made for their education. But disabled children were considered distinct from their peers. They were considered to be incapable of receiving education in general schools. Thus, for the first time, special schools and institutions were established in different countries for the education and training of such children. They were educated in special schools being separated from their parents and their non-disabled peers.

In the second half of the twentieth century, new thinking and new realizations have opened new directions for education of disabled children. It is now realised that a disabled child is not a different kind of person. He is a child with special needs. Like all other members of the society, the disabled must have the same rights to education, work and full participation in the society. It is also recognised that the disabled, particularly those with mild to moderate degree of disability and the orthopaedically handicapped, can be educated alongwith their non-disabled peers in general schools with provision for extra help. Moreover, education of disabled children in common with non-disabled children in general schools has been found to be an economical system in terms of expenses and coverage. These realizations, recognition and thinking on the part of educationists, planners and teachers have led to the conceptualisation of integrated education for the disabled children.

2. What is Integrated Education?

Integrated education movement flows directly from the recognition of equal rights for all citizens and equal educational opportunity for all children. It is based on the contention that while disabled children are children with special needs, their education should be provided in the least restrictive and most effective environment. The least restrictive environment which disabled children need can only be provided in general schools. Thus, integrated education refers to education of disabled children in common with others in general schools with provision for extra help for the disabled. It refers to integrating the physically and mentally handicapped children with the non-disabled children in regular classroom and providing specialised services to meet their special needs.

Integrated education is the outcome of significant modification in strategies related to the planning and delivery of services to the disabled. These significant modifications are :

— from protection to emancipation

— from wardship to independence

— from separation to integration

— from exclusion to inclusion

— from restriction to expansion

	Least Restrictive Educational Setting
Level A	Full time Regular Classroom attendance with Resource Teacher Support.
Level B	Regular Classroom attendance plus Part time Resource Room Support.
Level C	Special Class with Integration.

Four key processes are important in integrated education :

Normalization, Deinstitutionalization, Mainstreaming, Inclusion.

(i) *Normalization* is the process of creating a learning and social environment as normal as possible for the exceptional child and adult.

(ii) *Deinstitutionalization* is the process of releasing as many exceptional children and adult as possible from the confinement of residential institutions into their local community.

(iii) *Mainstreaming* is the process of bringing exceptional children into daily contact with non-exceptional children in an educational setting.

(iv) *Inclusion* is the process of bringing exceptional children of whatever condition into the general classroom for their education.

Integration is the opposite of segregation. Segregation is the process by which a special group in society is identified and gradually the social and physical distance between this group and the rest increases. A feeling of *otherness* develops in the group which alienates the former group. Integration is the process of bringing the 'part' (the handicapped) to the 'whole' (the society). The indicators of integration are that (i) handicapped persons enjoy the same right as the rest; (ii) have equal opportunity for growth and development in environmental conditions available to the rest; (iii) have access to the quality of life like any other citizen and (iv) are treated as equal partners in the community. The process begins by physical proximity, *i.e.*, reduction of physical distance. It continues with mutual sharing of the physical facilities and progresses towards reduction of social distance. The reduction of the physical and social distance results in social integration in which the groups become equal partners in the community.

3. Mechanics/Nature of Integrated Education

(i) Integrated education is an educational setting in which disabled children receive education alongwith non-disabled children in the regular classroom with provision for extra help for the disabled. Thus, integrated education is a practical solution to the problem of segregation of disabled children.

(ii) Integrated education is not an alternative to special education. Rather it is complementary to special education. Only mildly and sometimes moderately handicapped children can be enrolled in integrated schools. Severely handicapped children who are enrolled in special schools can also be admitted in integrated schools after they acquire communication skills, daily living skills, study skills, and other pre-requisite skills.

(iii) It is designed to provide equal educational opportunity to the disabled and to prepare them for independent living like other members of the society.

(iv) It provides the least restrictive and the most effective environment to disabled children so that they may grow and develop like other children.

(v) It is an educational setting which promotes a healthy social relationship between the disabled and the non-disabled children at all levels and reduces the physical distance between them through equal participation in social activities.

(vi) It is an arrangement in which disabled children are considered as important as their non-disabled peers.

(vii) It accepts the disabled child as an individual in his own rights.

(viii) In ensures civic rights to the disabled in order to raise their standards of living.

(ix) It is an economic system for the education of disabled children and solves the psychological problems which these children face in special educational settings.

(x) It is based on cooperative efforts of regular classroom teacher, the specialist teacher, parents and community members.

(xi) It is a viable approach to attain the goals of universalisation of elementary education by providing equality of educational and development opportunities to the disabled who were denied equality so far.

4. Scope of Integrated Education

Integrated education is proposed to provide educational facilities to the following types of disabled children.

(i) Children with locomotor handicap (orthopaedically handicapped).

(ii) Mildly and moderately hearing impaired.

(iii) Partially sighted children including one-eyed children.

(iv) Educable mentally retarded.

(v) Children with multiple handicaps (blind and orthopaedic, hearing impaired and orthopaedic, EMR and orthopaedic, visually impaired and hard of hearing).

(vi) Children with learning disability.

(vii) Blind children who have completed preparation in braille reading and writing, orientation and mobility training.

(viii) Deaf children who have acquired communication skills and learnt speech reading.

The scope of integrated education includes pre-school training for the disabled, counselling for parents, primary education, secondary education, +2 level of education, and vocational courses.

5. Educational Provisions

There are children with some impairment who can be educated in general schools with the existing facilities by general teachers without any formal training or preparation. There are children with certain impairments who can be educated in general schools with some preparation and slight modifications/adjustments/adaptations in teaching methods and materials. There are also a limited number of children with disabilities who will require comparatively prolonged formal preparation before they are educated in general schools.

Children with different types and levels of disability will require educational provisions matched with their needs. The educational provisions may be considered on the basis of the extent of their participation in educational activities in common with other children. The educational provisions in general schools will be as follows :

(i) *General classroom in general schools* : Disabled children receive education in the general classroom in general schools with other children. They are taught by general teachers. For example, children with locomotor disabilities, visual impairment with correction, mild hearing impairment and cases of marginally low intellectual functioning follow the same curriculum as their non-disabled peers.

(ii) *Education in general schools with adaptations and modifications of curriculum transaction* : The disabled child receives education in general schools in the general classroom following the same curriculum as others. However, adaptations of teaching techniques or materials according to his specific needs are made by the general teacher. This is specifically applied to low vision children, such cases of hearing impairment where hearing can be corrected through aids and, children with learning disabilities.

(iii) *Education in general classroom with support from special teacher* : Where the general class teacher has instructional or behavioural problems with the disabled child, he can seek the help of the special education teachers for instructional adaptation and modification. The special education teacher suggests educational alternatives to general class instruction. Thus, the disabled child receives services without being moved to a special class/or resource room through guidance from the special teacher.

(iv) *Education in general classroom with part-time withdrawal for special instruction* : A disabled child, though still in a general class setting, receives special part time instruction through a special teacher. For example, a child may need special assistance in reading or require extra time for a particular curriculum area. The child may go to a special teacher for between one and three class period(s) a day according to his need. For example, a blind child may go for special practice in language-learning.

(v) *Education in special class in general schools* : Some disabled children need full-time special class placement (self-contained class) to receive appropriate individualised instruction. It may be specifically required for severe and profound cases of hearing impairment and mentally retarded children. For example, mentally-retarded children may work in an integrated setting for non-academic activities like music, painting, and drama and may attend a special class for academic activities. Their curriculum is also different.

The educational provision described above indicates that special support can be provided for these children in a general classroom. For some children, however, these facilities will have to be provided in a resource room/centre where children with specific difficulties for which help cannot be extended in the general classroom are given instruction by the special teacher (resource/itinerant teacher).

(vi) *Preparation for education in general schools* : Severely handicapped children can benefit from education in general schools when they have the necessary communication skills, orientation and mobility skills (for blind children) and access to the school. Severely handicapped Children get such preparation in the home and ECCE centres, pre-schools attached to general schools, preschools and parent counselling centres, and special schools. Those children who have completed their preparation can be educated in general schools.

(vii) *Compensatory aids and appliances* : As discussed earlier some disabled children need special aids and appliances to compensate for their deficiencies. General schools admitting disabled children should arrange to provide the following aids and appliances.

For orthopaedically handicapped children

Adjustable furniture

Special writing material (thick pen)

Artificial limbs

Wheel chairs and crutches

For blind children

Braille slate and stylus, braille sheets

Abacus

Taylor frame

Mobility canes

Cassette and talking books

Braille text books

Bulletin board

Flat desks

Embossed graph sheets with rubber band and push pin tactile maps

Concrete objects to teach shape, size, thickness, weight, ascending and descending, etc. number, texture and motor coordination.

For partially-sighted and low vision children

Magnifying glass

Spectacles

Portable reading lamps

White board in place of black board

Large print materials.

For hearing impaired children

Hearing aid (group hearing aid and individual hearing aid) Speech trainer or voice trainer.

Mirror (big and small)

Special learning materials like flash cards, educational games and toy materials, hand-outs of classroom instruction.

For mentally retarded and learning disabled children

Educational games and play materials

Concrete objects for teaching different concepts

Picture cards and pictures

Day, Date and Month Calender

Tool box

Aids for sensory-motor coordination

Alternate learning materials (simplified).

6. Importance of Integrated Education

Education of the disabled in common with others is justified for the following reasons :

(i) The Programme of Action (NPE, 1986) indicated that out

of 12 million disabled persons, 4.3 million comprise of UPE age group. To this may be added 1.4 million in the earlier age group which has relevance for early identification and preparation for education. But these children are so scattered throughout the country that at any point of time in any place the number of disabled children is very neligible to warrant establishment of special schools for them.

Due to lack of adequate facilities for the education of disabled children, the enrolment of disabled children is very low even in special schools. A large number of such children are also out of school unidentified. These factors suggest identifying, assessing, and educating these disabled children in common with others in general schools.

(ii) With limited infrastructure for identification and inadequate facilities for their education, a large number of disabled children do enter the general schools. Due to lack of sensitivity to their needs in the school system, they experience learning problems and drop out. The exact magnitude of such drop-outs is not available but it is expected to be high. A systematic procedure of identification and assessment of their disability, qualitative improvement of education in schools, training of specialist teachers and provision of specialised help in integrated schools will ensure higher retention and lower drop-out rate among disabled children.

(iii) Once a child is placed in a special school, teachers tend to have low expectations of academic abilities of even mild and moderately disabled children with the result that their attainments fail to reach the optimum level owing to self-fulfilling prophecy. Even gifted handicapped children also fail to perform well in special schools. Integrated education, through the improved school atmosphere, and greater concern for the needs of disabled children, will tend to decrease the effects of self-fulfilling prophecy.

(iv) Education in common with others also provides a natural environment for interaction with non-disabled peers, to learn to cope with the environment, to accept, and to be accepted by their peers, to adjust emotionally to their personal capacity, to acquire a sense of competency and independence, and above all for socialisation.

(v) It is desirable that the scanty resources available for education should be fully utilised. Thus, for economic reasons, a large number of disabled children can be educated in common with others. As education in special schools is very costly, this facility has to be used only for those whose needs cannot be met in general schools.

(vi) In a UNESCO study conducted in 1985 involving fourteen countries the teachers teaching in general schools are reported to have expressed the opinion that they can teach children with certain disabilities with additional training input and organisational support.

7. The NPE (1986) and the POA relating to Integrated Education

The NPE (1986) underlines the fact that despite the enormous expansion of primary education in the post-independence period, the population of disabled children has not been adequately served as a part of UPE. Outlining the steps for ensuring equal educational opportunity for the handicapped the NPE states that the objective should be to integrate the physically and mentally handicapped with the general community, to prepare them for normal growth, and to enable them to face life with courage and confidence. It envisages that :

(i) Wherever possible education of children with locomotor handicap and other mild handicaps will be common with that of others. The children with severe handicaps are proposed to be enrolled in special schools with hostels at district headquarters.

(ii) As education in special schools is very costly, it will be ensured that only those children whose needs cannot be met in common schools are enrolled in these schools. As soon as the disabled children enrolled in special schools acquire the communication skills and study skills, they will be integrated into common schools. It is assumed that with the improved efficiency of the common school system the capacity of the common schools to cater to the needs of the disabled children will also improve.

(iii) Since special schools are costly and preparation of special teachers and other specialists will take time efforts should be made to increase enrolment of language handicapped and other mildly handicapped children and their retention in common schools by 25 per cent each year during the current plan period.

(iv) To achieve the above purpose (iii) the POA envisages the following steps :

Organising advocacy programme for administrators and teachers in the common school system.

Training of teachers on the management of disabled children.

Orientation of administrators.

Providing supervisory services to the teachers managing this group of children.

Developing alternative learning materials for children and teachers' handbook.

Supplying additional materials/equipment to the school.

Developing psychological services for the assessment of disability.

Mobilising support from other departments such as health, industry, social welfare and voluntary organisations.

(v) The following provisions including incentive have been proposed in the POA :

Provision of aids and appliances in the area to be covered.

Adequate provision for the payment of transportation allowance (Rs. 50 per month).

Provision for capital cost for the purchase of school rickshaw in rural areas to an institution which has at least 10 handicapped children.

Removal of architectural barriers in school building where at least 13 handicapped children are enrolled.

Supply of textbooks and uniform free of cost as given to S.C. and S.T. students.

Attendance incentives as given to girls and S.T. children.

Arrangement for the preparation of these children in early childhood centres for education in schools.

Provision for admission of children older than the eligibility (upto 8-9 years instead of 6 years).

8. Mainstreaming

What is Mainstreaming? The concept of mainstreaming owes its origin in the work and ideas of Samuel Gridley Howe, an American Physician, who took keen interest in the education of blind and deaf children. As early as 1851, Howe had stressed that blind children should be educated in regular schools because of the social advantages of such a setting. He was advocating in favour of "exposing the disabled to an educational experience as close to that of non-disabled as possible". In other words he was advocating in favour of mainstreaming the handicapped children in the general schools. It was in 1975 that the concept of mainstreaming was introduced in the "Education for All the Handicapped Act (USA)."

Mainstreaming refers to an educational placement procedure and process in which disabled children are educated in the least restrictive environment to satisfactorily provide for their educational and related needs. The concept of mainstreaming is based on the conviction that :

(i) Disabled children have a wide range of special educational needs.

(ii) The special educational needs of disabled children vary greatly in intensity and duration.

(iii) There is a continuum of educational settings which may be appropriate for an individual child's needs.

(iv) Disabled children should be educated with non-disabled children.

(v) Special classes, special schools and other ways of segregating the disabled from the non-disabled may be necessary only when the special needs of disabled children cannot be satisfied in general schools even with the provision of supplementary aids and services.

According to Kauffman et al (1975) "Mainstreaming refers to the temporal, instructional and social integration of eligible exceptional children with normal peers based on an ongoing, individually determined, educational planning and programming process and requires clarifications of responsibility among regular and special education, administrative, instructional and supportive personnel."

Components of Mainstreaming. According to this operational definition, there are three components of mainstreaming :

(i) Integration

(ii) Educational Planning and Programming.

(iii) Clarification of Responsibilities.

Integration : Integration is the opposite of segregations. Segregation is the process by which children with special needs or the disabled children are identified as a separate group and are educated in special schools in the company of other disabled children of the same category being alienated from the parents, siblings, non-disabled peers and their own community. Gradually the social and physical distance between this group and the rest increases. A feeling of 'otherness' develops in the group. Integration is the process of bringing the 'parts' (the handicapped children) to the 'whole' (the society). The indicators of integration are that disabled children enjoy the same right as the rest, have equal opportunity for growth and development in the least restrictive and most effective environment, have access to the quality of life like any other children, and are treated as equal partners in the school and community. The process begins by reduction of physical distance. It continues with mutual sharing of the physical facilities and proceeds towards reduction of social distance. The reduction of the physical and social distance results in social integration in which the groups become equal partners in the community.

Integration is basic to mainstreaming. Integration should be temporal, instructional and social. The child with special needs should be placed in a regular class with other children for a period of time which may vary from two periods to six periods every day. Along with temporal integration there should be social and instructional integration. The special child should be accepted by his peers, regular teachers and should participate in all social activities of the school. Instructional integration is the most difficult component for mainstreaming. The special child's instruction should be so designed that he participates in classroom activities with normal peers yet does not have difficulties in learning. The efficacy of mainstreaming depends in part upon the amount of time the special child spends in the regular classroom, the extent to which he is accepted by normal peers and participates in social activities, and the success of instruction in the regular classroom.

Educational planning and programming : Simply placing the special child in the regular classroom with other children is not enough for mainstreaming to succeed. The educational programme of the mainstreamed child needs to be planned carefully. Special efforts must be made to plan the programme for the unique needs of such children so that they can achieve the maximum benefits of participation in the regular classroom. For this to occur, supportive personnel and services should be provided both to the child and the regular class teacher.

Clarification of responsibilities : In some mainstreaming situations the regular teacher must assume total responsibility for the special child. But usually resource teachers are appointed in mainstreaming situations. When both regular teachers and the resource teacher are working with the child, there may be confusion regarding who is responsible for what. The child's total needs can be met when their respective roles are clearly and carefully delineated. The efficacy of mainstreaming depends upon both the regular teacher and the resource teacher discharging their respective responsibilities sincerely.

Efficacy of Mainstreaming. In summarizing what has been discussed above it can be said that the efficacy of mainstreaming depends on the following conditions :

(i) There should be temporal, social and instructional integration of handicapped children.

(ii) Educational programmes for the mainstreamed handicapped children should be planned carefully to meet their special educational needs.

(iii) Supportive services and personnel should be provided both to the children and the regular class teacher.

(iv) The responsibilities of the regular teacher and the resource teacher should be clearly delineated.

(v) The regular class teacher should ultimately take the responsibility of educating the handicapped children in the general school.

(vi) Only mildly handicapped children should be exposed to mainstreaming situation. Severely handicapped children who have completed their preparation and learnt the pre-academic skills, daily living skills, communication skills, and other pre-requisite skills in special school settings may be later mainstreamed in the general schools.

(vii) The regular teachers must accept and agree to implement mainstreaming in their classrooms and schools.

(viii) The regular teachers must prepare themselves for their new and difficult role. The authorities must arrange to provide inservice and pre-service training on characteristics and special educational needs of handicapped children to the regular teachers.

(ix) In all cases parents should be involved in the care, training, and placement of their handicapped children.

9. Issues in Integration

Integrated education for disabled children is a fast growing field. In a new area like IED issues, concerns and controversies are bound to occur. In this field, new trends are taking place from time to time. Each time a new trend develops, it evolves into an issue and another new trend eventually takes its place. Some issues relate to factors over which we have little or no control. Some issues relate to questions which we may not answer in the next hundred years or ever. For example, we may never fully understand how the mind functions, how children learn. Our knowledge about children's behaviour, particularly of disabled children, remains incomplete, partial, and hypothetical. With this limited knowledge and hypothetical data we are teaching disabled children in common with others in the regular classroom. Thus, issues are inevitable. Some of the common issues in integration are as follows :

(i) Education of disabled children in common schools has become very popular in our country. Parents have demanded this programme so much that the number of IED schools in the state of Orissa has increased from 20 in the year 1987 to 143 in the year 1992. The critical issue is not opening of new IED schools but the fact that parents demand instant and simple solutions to incredibly complex problem of teaching their children all the academic skill, social skills, vocational skills and daily-living skills. Disabled children, in most cases, are identified late. In most cases also they come to the school with no or very little home training. Teaching these children the skills required for social, academic, vocational and independent living will take time.

(ii) Another issue relates to their categorisation. There are various categories or types of handicap and also different degrees of handicap. The issue is "Are they real, specific and individually discrete categories?"

Part of the difficulty relates to the manner in which we have attempted to define each category so that it can be identified as separate or different from other category. This is not so significant with respect to severe levels of disability like blindness or deafness. However, disabled children who are educated in general schools are those with-mild-to-moderate levels of disability. These levels of disability lead to confusion with respect to correct identification as a result of which many non-disabled children with almost similar characteristics due to environmental factors and instructional failures are also identified, purposefully or due to ignorance, as disabled and enrolled in the scheme. Our interpretation of mild and moderate levels of disability is based on incomplete and tentative conclusions.

(iii) Related to the above issue is the question relating to tests, techniques and personnel required for assessment of disabled children. The scheme of IED envisages that all disabled children should be properly assessed by competent authority. Assessment is needed for two purposes — to determine the type and level of disability and to provide guidance for intervention. The question is : "which tests and what techniques are to be used for assessment?" Another question is 'who should conduct assessment?"

The tests and techniques used at present are subject to various degrees of bias. Very often tests are not readily available for use by assessment personnel. Again assessment — medical or psychological — is not always possible, particularly in rural areas due to non-availability of specialist doctors and psychologists. For these reasons many disabled children are enrolled in the IED schools and are provided with facilities and incentives although they remain unassessed for the total period of their school education. This defeats the very purpose of the scheme of IED. As a temporary alternative to this difficulty the concept of "functional assessment" has been developed by NCERT, New Delhi. Even functional assessment is also not adopted in most of the IED schools.

(iv) The question of "how do children learn" or "what factors inhibit learning" is still a major issue. We know that children need to be exposed to a board range of spoken language so that they will be able to learn and develop adequate spoken language. This is why deaf children who do not experience a broad range of spoken language have considerable difficulty in developing adequate language. But what about children with normal hearing, normal mental ability and normal exposure to language who do not learn normally? Why and how is their language learning inhibited? What are the factors that lead to their learning difficulties? Though we know some of the factors that are essential to normal learning, there are some we simply do not understand: Thus, we may conclude that we do not know enough about how disabled and non-disabled children learn and what factors inhibit their learning. With this partial knowledge we are intervening in the education and training of disabled children. This is certainly a major issue for teachers teaching disabled children.

(v) The scheme of IED envisages that hundred per cent financial assistance will be provided by the Central Government to State and Union Territories for providing education to disabled children in general schools. States and Union Territories have also identified general schools to implement the scheme of IED. But what will happen if the Central Government with-holds this financial grant? Will the State Governments bear all expenses for the education of the disabled in general schools if the Central Government stops giving grant? What is the future of the scheme of IED? At present, due to financial constraints the State Government is not in a position to releases the salary to teachers regularly. The disabled children are also not getting financial assistance regularly and in time. They have to wait until Central Government releases the grant. If the Central Government stops giving grant the State Government may not be in a position to bear all expenses. But if we have to provide equal rights to disabled children, the State Government has to frame its policy in clear and categorical terms regarding implementation of IED in general schools even when central assistance is not available.

(vi) In pursuance of the present policy of the State Government some schools have started enrolling mild-to-moderately handicapped children in their regular classrooms. The issue is; Are they receiving the special help they need for maximization of their potentialities? We have formulated the minimum levels of learning (MLL) in respect of various subjects which every learner is expected to acquire. The question is : Should the disabled learner, particularly the mentally retarded, the visually impaired, the hearing impaired and the learning disabled also learn the MLL? If yes, are they trained by the teachers to acquire the MLL? Excepting few cases, most disabled children enrolled in different IED units are deprived of the special help they need. They are at best given 'some education' which they were deprived of earlier. In view of the no detention policy they are promoted year after year to the next grade without considering whether they have acquired the MLL specified for a particular grade. This is also true in case of normal children. New IED units are attached to primary schools, disabled children are enrolled in those units; but provision for special help is not made in those schools. The persons who are appointed as resource teachers are not qualified, specially trained and competent to provide special help to those who need it. Graduates with special education background remain unemployed or at best employed with a meagre salary but Matriculates with no background in special education are employed as resource teachers. When such teachers are underqualified to teach normal children how can they be expected to provide specialised instruction to disabled children? This is a very crucial issue which calls for modification of recruitment practices by the appointing authority.

(vii) Another issue relates to the mode of examination. Disabled children, particularly the visually impaired, the hearing impaired and the mentally retarded, who are supposed to be exposed to the same curricular experiences have to pass the common examination held at the end of instruction in a particular grade or level. Although they need a different mode and additional time to respond to test items in view of their special needs, they are not granted the privilege. Thus, such children fail to demonstrate their talents although they are capable of doing that. Special regulations have been passed by the examining boards and councils for disabled children enrolled in special schools. Similar concessions should also be granted to disabled children enrolled in general schools.

(viii) Another critical issue in the process of integration is labeling. It is observed that once some children are identified as disabled they are categorised and labelled as MR or LD or deaf or one-eyed or crippled. Such labeling creates a feeling of unworthiness among those labelled and the society, parents, and teachers get biased in their expectations. Particularly teacher's expectations are reflected in children's performances. The recent trend is moving away from labeling and getting closer and closer towards non-categorical special education.

(ix) A fundamental question in integrated education is : How can one resource teacher teach different subjects to several disabled children studying in different classes? It is, no doubt, difficult on the part of one resource teacher to teach all subjects to all disabled children in all classes. But as per the recent trend, the major responsibility for teaching disabled children in integrated settings rests with the general teacher as for other children. The resource teacher act as a consultant to the general teachers in adapting instructional materials and methods to the specific needs of the disabled child. He does not teach the disabled child directly. His responsibility is to provide specialised instruction in the resource room. His direct role decreases as the disabled child moves up to higher grades.

(x) At present, primary schools implementing the scheme of IED admit disabled children belonging to different categories — visually impaired, hearing impaired, mentally retarded and learning disabled. Such schools get the services of a resource teacher having special education background in any one area of disability. He is expected to teach all categories of disabled children in the resource room. The question is : can one resource teacher render special assistance to all children belonging to different areas of disability? A teacher trained to teach hearing impaired children may not do justice when he is asked to teach MR children. Similarly a teacher trained to teach MR children may not be able to teach visually impaired children. What is the solution then? This question relates to the possibility of having multi-category teachers. If the quality of multi-category teachers, training can be controlled, such teachers can be expected to render special assistance to disabled children of various categories.

4

Integrating the Hearing Impaired

1. What is Hearing Impairment?

Hearing impairment refers to a defect in or damage to the hearing mechanism. This defect or damage may occur in any part of the ear — outer ear or middle ear or inner ear. Hearing impairment leads to hearing disability or loss of hearing. Hearing disability or loss of hearing may range in severity from mild to moderate to profound. A person may become deaf or hard-of-hearing depending upon the nature of impairment and the degree of hearing loss.

A child may be born with some impairment in the hearing mechanism or the impairment may occur after birth due to infection, disease and obstruction or damage due to accident. Due to hearing impairment the child becomes unable to hear, speak and acquire language. Thus, a child may become dumb largely because he is deaf.

2. Classification of Hearing Impaired

The hearing impaired children have been classified under various sub-groups from various angles.

(a) Classification based on the degree of hearing loss. Depending on the degree of hearing loss the hearing impaired children are classified into two groups such as the deaf, and the hard-of-hearing.

The total inability to hear is called deafness. The deaf are those who, even with the best auditory training, cannot learn to understand speech mainly through hearing. The hard-of-hearing children have some residual degree of hearing and can be benefited through amplification. They are those children in whom the sense of hearing, although defective, is functional with or without a hearing aid.

The hearing impaired children are also classified into the following five sub-groups depending on the degree of hearing loss or hearing sensitivity. Hearing loss or hearing sensitivity is measured in decibels (dB).

Hearing impairment categories based on the degree of hearing loss as per the Ministry of Welfare (Govt. of India), Notification No. 4283HW, dt. 6.8.86 are given in the following Table :

Category	Type of Impairment	dB Level in better ear	Percentage of impairment
I	Mild	dB 26 to 40	Less than 40%
II	Moderate	dB 41 to 55	40% — 50%
III	Severe	dB 56 to 70	50% — 75%
IV	Profound	dB 71 to 90	75% — 100%
	Near total deafness	dB 91 and above	100%
	Total deafness	No hearing	100%

Decibels (dB) means a unit of relative loudness of a sound. Zero decibels (O dB) designates the point at which people with normal hearing can detect even the faintest sound. Each succeeding number of dB indicates a certain degree of hearing loss. Decibels are found from audiograms. An audiogram is a graphic representation of the weakest sound that the individukal being tested can hear at each of several different levels of pitch (Hz).

(b) Classification based on age of onset. Hearing impairment may occur since birth or it may be acquired at any age in life. Thus, depending on the age of onset we have two groups of hearing impaired children such as,

Congenitally deaf

Adventitiously deaf

The congenitally deaf child is one who is born with impaired hearing. Such a child has not heard any sound or speech. The adventitiously deaf child is one who is born with normal hearing. He has acquired speech, but later lost hearing ability due to infection, disease or some damage to the hearing mechanism.

(c) Classification based on language experience. Hearing impaired children are also classified into the following two groups depending upon the language experience they have acquired :

Pre-lingual deaf

Post-lingual deaf

The prelingual deaf child is one who is born with little or no hearing. He has suffered the loss of hearing early in infancy before speech and language patterns are acquired. Post-lingual deaf children are those who had language exposure for some time but later they became deaf owing to environmental factors. The speech of pre-lingual deaf child is slow and laboured and is usually accompanied by a high pitch. Prolonged vowels, rhythmic abnormality, excessive nasality, imperfect joining of consonants and defective articulation are some of the characteristics of their speech.

(d) Classification based on the location of the problem. Hearing loss is also classified into three types depending upon the location of the hearing problem or defect. These are —

Conductive loss,
Sensorineural loss and
Mixed loss.

If the hearing problems are located in the outer ear and the middle ear it is called conductive loss. If the problems arise out of the defects in the inner ear it is called sensori-neural loss. Conductive loss of hearing is easier to correct than sensori-neural loss. A combination of conductive loss and sensori-neural loss is called mixed loss.

(e) Central deafness. In addition to the above types of hearing loss there is another type of hearing loss called the central deafness. When the sound vibrations reach the inner ear, the inner ear transforms these vibrations and sends them to the auditory centre in the brain. The brain perceives these sounds meaningfully and understands the message. If there is any defect in the auditory centre in the brain we cannot hear anything. This type of hearing loss is known as central deafness.

Among all these classifications the one based on the degree of hearing loss — Mild, Moderate, Severe and Profound — is widely accepted for integrated education purposes. Children with mild to moderate loss of hearing can be integrated in regular schools.

3. Identification and Placement of Hearing Impaired

Need for Early Identification

The hearing impaired children should be identified as early as possible by parents in the home and later by teachers in the school. Early identification is important for the following reasons :

(i) Early identification will lead to early diagnosis of the degree of hearing loss and his residual hearing.

(ii) Early identification and diagnosis will help in obtaining a suitable hearing aid and beginning auditory training and speech training which will make the child's langauge and speech almost normal. This will also reduce the effect of the handicap on his development.

(iii) Early identification and intervention will help in better exposure to language experience and thus better psycho-social adjustment and educational achievement.

(iv) Unless hearing impariment is detected early and intervention programmes are initiated early, habilitation will not be fruitful. Thus, early identification and intervention are the key to prevention of speech and language defects caused by hearing impairment.

Methods of identification : There are various methods employed for early identification of hearing impaired children. They fall mostly into one of the following categories.

(i) High risk register.

(ii) Screening procedure.

(iii) Objective measurement.

In the high risk register, information on all risk factors that may cause hearing handicap in the child are collected with the help of a questionnaire from the mother. Children who present risk factors are followed up and studied by audiologists. This is a health-related identification procedure used by volunteers who are trained by audiologists. In the screening technique behavioural observation is used for observing the child's responses and reflexes to the given sounds at various frequencies, distance and loudness. Objective measurement is based on sophisticated technology which costs a lot of money.

The methods mentioned above are mostly used in developed countries. They are very expensive methods and are not used in India. Most of these methods are useful for identifying severely and profoundly hearing impaired children. They are not practically useful for parents and class room teachers. Parents, particularly the mothers, have a major role to play in observing the behaviour of infants and children at different periods and referring the suspected cases to the audiologists and ENT specialists for systematic observation. Thus observation of infants' behaviour and responses to different sounds at different periods of their life is more useful and practicable than other methods.

A large number of mildly and moderately hearing imparied children do enter the regular schools. But they remain unidentified as having any degree of hearing impairment. Their problems go unnoticed and unattended and at times misunderstood as a result of which such children experience failure in academic and social situations. They drop-out from the school before completing elementary education. This has implications for regular teachers. Regular teachers can play a significant role in identifying hearing impaired children by observing their behavioural characteristics. The following check list developed by the NCERT, New Delhi will help teachers to identify hearing impaired children in the school.

Identification check-list for the hearing impaired

— Does the child ask for repetition of instruction?

— Does the child display restlessness and inattention?

— Does the child have any observable deformity of the ear?

— Does the child have a discharge from the ear?

— Does the child complain of pain in the ear frequently?

— Does the child turn his head frequently in order to hear better?

— Is the child unable to follow your instruction?

— Does the child scratch his ear frequently?

— Does the child focus on the speaker's face while listening to understand speech?

— Does the child ask for help from fellow students in taking notes when the teacher explains verbally in the classroom?

If answers to four or five questions are marked 'yes' the teacher can suspect hearing impairment in the child. Such a child should be referred to the audiologist and ENT specialist for systematic investigation and assessment. If the assessment report indicates mild or moderate degree of hearing impairment the child can be integrated in the regular school without much difficulty. If the assessment report indicates severe or profound hearing loss the child should be placed in a special school for the deaf.

Placement. Placement of the hearing impaired child should be based on the assessment report. Placement refers to placing a child in an institution — home or any educational institution where systematic and orderly arrangements are ensured for proper care, training and development of the child. The following are some of the placement programmes for the hearing impaired :

(i) Home-based programme.

(ii) Special school placement.

(iii) Part-time special school placement.

(iv) Placement in integrated settings.

(v) Vocational placement.

Home-based programme : Home-based programme is ideal for very young infants. If a young infant is suspected by parents and later confirmed by the ENT specialist and audiologist as hearing-impaired, parents can do a lot to help the infant to overcome the effect of his disability as he grows older. Parents can provide a stimulating environment using indigenous materials and every day situations. They can provide auditory training, speech and language stimulation to the young infant in the home. The young child can be encouraged to use the hearing aid. Parents can provide corrective exercises to the child in the home. Home-based programme is purely an individualised training programme which will vary from child to child depending upon the nature of the child's impairment, his general development pattern, and degree of parental involvement or interaction with the child.

Special school placement : Special school placement is required for (1) severely hearing-impaired children (ii) children who are detected late, and (iii) children who cannot be trained by parents in the home. There are special schools for the deaf where these three types of children can be placed for intervention programmes. In special schools for the deaf the standard curriculum followed in regular schools may also be followed for those who can take it comfortably. If necessary, the curriculum may be altered for those who cannot keep pace with the normal school curriculum.

Part-time special class (resource room) placement : There are many hearing-impaired children who show some capacity to profit from regular classroom teaching. They only need adequate academic preparation at least in some subject areas, adequate personal-social maturity and motivation levels and at least reasonable communication skills. Such children can attend a half-day in a regular school and spend the remaining half of the day in a special class or resource room. In the resource room the special teacher can help the child with the academic work he cannot cope within the regular class. In the resource room situation the teacher can work as much as is needed on a one-to-one basis with the child. Once ready, the child can be gradually reintegrated for greater periods of time into the regular classroom. Resource room placement is gaining popularity day by day.

Placement in the integrated school : There are some hearing impaired children who have adequate motivation. They have acquired reasonable communication skills and academic preparation. These children and the mildly hearing-impaired children can be placed in integrated schools to be educated in common with others.

However, whatever placement programmes may be followed for a particular hearing-impaired child, the child should be assessed periodically to ascertain the progress made by him and to suggest measures to help the child overcome his difficulties.

Vocational placement : Vocational placement is required for older adolescents and young adults. Vocational training is to be given to the hearing impaired child depending on his level of intelligence, area of interest, aptitude, level of maturity and adaptability and communication skills. Vocational education may begin from the senior secondary level or +2 stage.

Among all these types of educational placement which one is relatively more beneficial? Most authorities agree that the specific needs of each child must be considered in any decision about placement of hearing impaired children. The extent of the child's hearing impairment, the amount of pre-school training or treatment he might have received, the capability of his parents to understand and implement these programmes, his readiness (or lack of it) to utilise various training strategies as well as his readiness to be integrated into a regular class setting—all these will effect in a major way the success or failure of an educational placement.

4. Characteristics of Hearing Impaired Children

Hearing loss can have profound consequences for some aspects of a person's behaviour and little or no effect on other characteristics. If you are asked to choose, "which would you rather be — blind or deaf?" most of your first reply will be to choose deafness, probably because of your reliance upon sight for mobility and because many of the beauties of nature are visual. In terms of functioning in a language and academically-oriented society, however, the deaf child is at a much greater disadvantage. The psychological and behavioural characteristics of the hearing impaired children are given below :

(a) Language and Speech Development

(i) The ability to learn language and speech is the most severely affected area of development of the hearing impaired.

(ii) Without extensive training, the hearing impaired child will not develop normal language.

(iii) Earlier the hearing loss occurs, the more pronounced the language deficit will be.

(iv) The child who is born totally deaf will grow up mute unless special training is initiated (Carhart, 1970).

(v) The attitude that deafness automatically leads to an inability to speak is not scientifically based.

(vi) While profound hearing impairment is a great barrier to normal language development, there are very few deaf individuals who cannot be taught some use of language.

(vii) There are cases of children with hearing losses as great as 70 to 90 dB in the better ear who have nevertheless developed excellent speech (Fry, 1966).

(viii) Children who lose hearing after having been exposed to the experience of speech, even for as short period as one year, can be trained much more easily in all language arts, even if formal training begins some years after they have become deaf.

The deaf child demonstrates a particular pattern of babbling as an infant. The deaf infant enters the babbling stage at the same time as the normal infant, but soon abandons. This is because he or she

— receives inadequate auditory feedback when he himself makes sounds;

— receives inadequate verbal reinforcement from adults;

— is unable to hear adequately an adult language model.

(b) Intellectual Ability

(i) Contrary to the popular notion, deaf children are found not necessarily slower in intellectual development than the normal children (Furth, 1961).

(ii) Thinking process of normal and deaf children are found to be similar (Furth, 1964, 1971).

(iii) The cognitive abilities of deaf children are essentially unimpaired except in those cases which involve language experience (Furth, 1961).

(iv) Deaf children who have not received adequate parental stimulation or educational instruction do perform less well than normals on intellectual tasks.

(v) Deaf children are retarded in intellectual tasks which require verbal skills. But in intellectual tasks which are primarily non-verbal in nature they are not found retarded.

(vi) Hearing impaired children get a higher score in non-verbal intelligence testing than in verbal intelligence testing.

(c) Academic Achievement

(i) Hearing impaired children are frequently handicapped in varying degree with regard to educational achievement.

(ii) They are particularly handicapped in reading which relies heavily upon language skills.

(iii) The gloomy picture of the academic progress of the hearing impaired, particularly the deaf, does not appear to be improving.

(iv) Only a small percentage of deaf individuals comprehend language well enough to read a college level textbook (Furth, 1973).

(v) The gloomy picture of the academic achievement of deaf children is mainly due to the fact that academic atmosphere in schools and colleges is predominantly verbal in nature and that the deaf children have deficiency in verbal skills.

(d) Social and Occupational Adjustment

(i) Social and personality characteristics of hearing impaired children are markedly different from the normal children.

(ii) Since social interaction depends upon communication and the hearing impaired children, particularly the deaf, have communication problems such chilrden have problems of social adjustment.

(iii) Because of their communication problems and failure in social interaction such children live in a world of isolation.

(iv) Such children have a strong desire for social interaction and social acceptance. But the hearing people do not accept them. This creates a sense of inferiority and frustration in the hearing impaired children.

(v) The hearing impaired children, thus, form a group of their own, an association of the deaf for their common interest and interaction.

(vi) A large majority of hearing impaired children are employed in jobs requiring manual work. Sometimes they are over qualified for a job in which they are placed. It is not clearly evident whether hearing impaired children can be successful in managerial and secretariat services, but the fact remains that employers do not prefer them for such jobs. But there is no reason why a hearing impaired person cannot succeed in occupations which do not demand verbal communication skills, particularly speaking ability.

(vii) The hearing impaired children are not different from the normal children in emotional adjustment. The same environmental factors which cause emotional disturbance in normal children also cause emotional disturbances in hearing impaired children.

All these characteristics are not necessarily to be found in all categories of hearing impaired children. The hearing impaired children may differ from each other in relation to these characteristics depending upon their degree of hearing loss and the age of onset of hearing loss.

(e) Other Characteristics

Some studies indicate that the hearing impaired child is inferior in intellectual ability, educational achievement and personal-social adjustment. These children score a relatively low score on IQ testing. In general their performance in academic subjects of the school is also poor. They face difficulty in personal-social adjustment. All these characteristics are mainly due to the fact that the hearing impaired child has not acquired the basic language and speech patterns which are required in intellectual functioning, academic success and social adjustments. This is particularly true in case of severely and profoundly impaired, cogenitally deaf, pre-lingually deaf and children with sensori-neural deafness. My experience shows that the mildly and moderately hearing-impaired children, children who had some language experience before they became deaf and children with conductive loss of hearing do better in IQ testing, educational achievements and social adjustment. They are immensely benefited from the use of hearing aid, auditory training and integrated education programmes, provided they are detected early and corrective measures are applied as early as possible.

5. Care and Training of Hearing Impaired

Hearing-impaired children differ from one another in many ways. They may differ in the degree and type of hearing loss, the age of onset of deafness, intelligence, parent's ability and attitude, home environment and the nature and amount of their home-training, if any. The care, training and education of such children, therefore, must depend on these factors mentioned above.

Every child, whether he is abled or disabled, has a right to education and every society must grant this right to the hearing-impaired children to receive appropriate training and education so that they become useful members of the society and participate in nation building instead of being a burden for the parents. The care and training of hearing-impaired children should match with their degree and type of loss. Moreover, care and training of hearing-impaired children should be the joint responsibility of the home, school, community, health and social welfare personnel.

Parents' responsibility : Care and training of a hearing impaired child should start in the home. Parents, siblings and other members of the family have a major and crucial role to play in the care and training of the disabled child. Since parents' responsibility in the care and training of hearing impaired children is beyond the scope of our discussion this will not be discussed in detail in this section. However, few hints are necessary here. Parents' responsibility lies in :

(i) Early identification of hearing impairment based on the child's developmental responses to sound and speech.

(ii) Referring the suspected cases to the ENT specialists and the audiologist for assessment.

(iii) Accepting the impaired child and showing love and affection to him like other normal children in the family.

(iv) Consulting the specialists and the teachers and sharing the responsibility for the training of the child.

(v) Encouraging the child to use the hearing aid regularly.

(vi) Teaching the child verbal skills, writing skills, reading skills and stimulating their language development.

(vii) Encouraging self-playing, playing with siblings, playing with the peer groups and developing singing, saying rhymes, listening to stories and the habit of sharing and taking turns.

(viii) Creating conditions for social normalisation of the child in the home.

(ix) Acting as per the advice of specialists.

(x) Preparing the child for integration in the school.

School's responsibility : In addition to parents' responsibility the school has a major responsibility in the care and training of hearing-impaired children. The major problem of hearing-impaired children lies in their deficiency in speech and language development and communication problem. There are three methods of training deaf children — the oral method, the manual method and the total communication approach. Finger spelling and sign language are examples of manual method. Lip reading or speech reading and auditory training are examples of oral method. The manual method is appropriate for severely and profoundly deaf children. The oral method is best suited for mild-to-moderately hearing handicapped children. Since hearing-impaired children who are enrolled in general schools are mostly mildly or moderately handicapped we will discuss lip reading and auditory training in detail. In addition to these, techniques of curriculum adaptation and teaching strategies should also be kept in mind.

(a) Sign Language.

The main problem faced by hearing impaired persons is effective communication. The speech of a profoundly deaf person is hardly intelligible to hearing persons. For this purpose sign language is extensively used by most of them. Sign language is a system of gestures that is used to convey general ideas or thoughts. There are a variety of sign languages. Today a standard set of signs known as American sign language (Ameslan) is used by many deaf people. Profoundly deaf children who have virtually an inability to communicate through verbal languages and whose speech is not intelligible should be trained to use non-verbal signs and gestures or more particularly the Ameslan. This is possible only by specially trained teachers in special schools.

(b) Finger Spelling.

Profoundly deaf children who have had some schooling and education can be taught finger spelling to achieve some facility in communication amongst themselves and also with the hearing-speaking world. This is inevitable since the speech of a profoundly deaf perosn is hardly intelligible to hearing person despite the fact that he may have acquired some language and is capable of using simple words or sentences.

Although educated deaf persons could communicate by resorting to writing, it is not practical to move around with paper and pencil all the time. Hence, the need arises for finger spelling. Finger spelling is nothing but writing in the air with configurations of fingers. The words for which there are no signs (such as names of persons) are often finger spelled. Thus, finger spelling can be described as a manual representation of written language. Put simply, finger spelling is the use of finger positions to represent the letters of the alphabet. Alphabet is a system of letters. To some extent finger spelling resembles the printed letters of the alphabet.

In India mainly two types of finger spelling are used. Both are based on English alphabet. Each letter (A to Z) has a distinct shape. The English finger spelling is performed either with one hand as in the American system, or with both hands as in the British system. The Indian Manual Alphabet named as "Kara Pallavi" has also been developed for use in Indian context. It is based on the American one-hand alphabet system.

When finger spelling, the palm of the hand should face the audience. The hand should not block a view of the lips as it is important to see lip movements as well. Ideally the words should be spelt at shoulder level. Finger spelling can be taught in special schools for the deaf.

(c) Speech Reading (Lip Reading).

Speech reading is sometimes referred to as lip reading. Lip reading refers to observing the lip mnovements or movement of the mouth of the speaker and understanding what is being told by the speaker. But in speech reading the deaf child not only observes the lip movements of the speaker but also uses the visual stimuli in the enviornment to comprehend spoken messages. Thus, speech reading is more comprehensive and a more accurate term than lip reading. The major goals of speech reading are :

(i) Observing the lip movements and facial expression of the speaker;

(ii) Observing the visual stimuli in the environment;

(iii) Understanding what is being spoken.

Principles of Speech Reading

(i) Teach the child to pay attention to and obtain meaning from the environment.

(ii) Teach the child to expect certain kinds of messages in certain kinds of situations.

(iii) Teach the child to associate specific movements of the mouth with specific sounds.

(iv) Relate your facial expressions directly to the content and tone of the words you are using.

(v) Engender in the child an awareness of his visual surrounding by showing the child pictures/objects and then asking questions about them.

(vi) Speak to the deaf or the hard-of-hearing child as often as possible.

(vii) Speak slowly.

(viii) Speak clearly.

(ix) Speak in a natural way without exaggeration.

(x) See that your face is clearly visible to the child.

(xi) See that your face is illuminated while you are speaking to the child.

(xii) Stand or sit in front of the child while you are speaking to him.

(xiii) Look at his face while you are speaking to him.

(xiv) Don't smoke or chew betels while speaking to the child.

(xv) Ensure that the matter you are talking about is known to the child.

(xvi) Don't speak loudly close to the hearing aid.

(d) Auditory Training.

The growing body of evidence supports the belief that almost no child is born with absolutely no hearing sensation. A hearing impaired child has some residual hearing ability. Auditory training is the procedure of teaching the deaf or hard-of-hearing child to make use of his residual hearing ability. It has three major goals :

(i) Development of awareness of a variety of sounds, including speech in his environment;

(ii) Development of the ability to make gross discriminations among non-verbal or environmental sounds;

(iii) Development of the ability to discriminate among speech sounds under high and low redundancy conditions (High redundancy refers to speech consisting of simple, familiar subject matter with little distraction from the environment. Low redundancy approximates more closely the way in which speech is used in the natural environment).

Principles of Auditory Training

(i) Formal auditory training is essential to teach the deaf child to make use of his remaining hearing ability.

(ii) The less severe the hearing loss, the more auditory training should be emphasized.

(iii) It is important to begin auditory training early.

(iv) Auditory training should better be provided with a hearing aid.

(v) Auditory training, even without a hearing aid, should be begun as soon as it is determined that a child is deaf.

(vi) Auditory training appears to be more effective through mutual reinforcement, when hearing is combined with vision and/or touch.

(vii) Auditory training should be geared to a child's auditory capabilities. This requires frequent assessment of his hearing capacity.

(viii) Auditory training should be based on experiences that are meaningful.

(e) The Total Communication Method

A recent development in the methodology of teaching communication skills to deaf children is the total communication method. This method combines all the means and methods — speech reading, finger spelling, sign language, auditory training, etc. The idea is to teach communication to the hearing impaired child by any means. The oral method or the manual method is not suitable to meet the needs of all hearing impaired children. Hence, instead of debating which method is more appropriate to a particular hearing impaired child a combination of different methods can ben adopted which will meet the needs of all hearing impaired children. This method is becoming very popular in various schools.

(f) Curriculum Adaptation and Teaching Strategies

The centrally sponsored scheme of IED visualises that the same learning experiences will be provided to both the disabled and the normal children studying in the IED schools. But hearing-impaired children, like other disabled children, have difficulty in understanding some of the content areas which include more verbal concepts. It is, therefore, necessary to adapt the curriculum to the needs and difficulties of such children. The following principles are important :

(i) While adapting the curriculum to the needs of hearing impaired children, the objectives of instruction should remain same for hearing-impaired and normal children. Only learning materials and methodology may be modified. The learning materials and methodology have to be modified in such a way that it will not disturb the majority of normal children studying in the class.

(ii) Ideally speaking the ratio between hearing impaired and normal children in a particular classroom should be 1 : 5 in Indian context. The hearing-impaired children should be asked to sit on the front benches/in the front line along with normal children. This will help them to hear better. If a hearing-impaired child has to sit on any side (left or right side) in the front line then the teacher must arrange to ensure that the better ear of the child is towards the class and the teacher.

(iii) In an integrated setting the normal peers are to be encouraged to participate in the education and training of hearing impaired. They can participate in correction of specific learning problems, teaching spelling, articulation, new concepts and curricular activities.

(iv) The teacher has to see that the hearing impaired child is using the hearing aid regularly in the class. He has also to check, from time to time, the working condition of the hearing aid.

(v) The hearing-impaired children need to develop adequate speech and language patterns. Supportive aids like recorded tapes, articulation charts, speech trainers, photo album, concrete objects and other visual cues should be used for speech training, speech correction and language learning.

Adjustment of material and methodology can also be done with resource room teaching. The teacher should identify the learning difficulty of the hearing-impaired subject-wise and suggest remedial exercises accordingly. These exercises should be organised by the resource teacher outside the class by a special arrangement of the time table within the normal school hour. For example, the hearing-impaired child may have difficulty in learning to speak certain sounds such as 'bh', 'th', 'dh', etc. and discriminate certain sounds. For developing sound discrimnination and teaching the child to speak certain sounds the resource teacher should give corrective exercises to the hearing impaired child in the resource room. Adequate training in speech correction with the help of speech trainer, recorded tapes, photo album and articulation chart in the resource room will be very useful.

Hearing impaired children have faulty patterns of language learning and usage. They generally have a misarticulation problem and as a result they also spell words wrongly. They generally write in the way they speak. For example, they may say and write ‘tigre’ for ‘tiger’ and ‘klass’ for ‘glass’. For correcting such problems, the teacher should give more visual cues on articulation of the sounds used for each word. This will help them to learn to speak and spell words correctly. The teacher may provide additional work book for writing. In addition to the above, the teacher should give emphasis on story telling, short question and answer method in the taching and learning of language and speech.

(vi) The hearing impaired children have difficulty in learning abstract concepts and difficult words. The wholistic method based on figures, pictures, and concrete experiences, audiovisual aids, role playing and dramatisation should be used for teaching new, difficult and abstract concepts. Action-oriented situations should be given for teaching emotional concepts like happiness, unhappiness, crying, shouting etc.

(vii) Hearing impaired children have the primary difficulty of learning language and speech. Since language learning is basic to learning all other subjects the hearing-impaired children, owing to their difficulty in learning langauge, have problems in learning other subjects. If the hearing impaired children can be helped to learn the language and speech patterns their problems in learning other subjects can be sorted out easily by the teacher.

(viii) The resource teacher should keep a record of what the child knows, what he can do and what he cannot do, plan his lessons according to the educational needs of the child, guide other teachers in teaching the various lessons, assess periodically the progress made by the child, encourage, motivate and provide feedback to the child regularly.

6. Role of Teacher

Managing hearing impaired children : The regular teacher may at one time or another have hard-of-hearing children in his class. He has an important role to play in managing such children in the class.

(i) There are behavioural characteristics or symptoms of hearing impairment which the regular classroom teacher should watch for. He should refer suspected cases or advise parents to consult with specialist doctors for medical treatment.

(ii) The very presence of one or two hearing-impaired children in the class of 35 to 40 hearing students is likely to create a feeling of uneasiness in the minds of the class teacher. If he has no previous knowledge of such children and their handicap he will ask himself, "How will I teach them?" Certainly they create a problem for him. He should, therefore, attend short-term training or orientation course so that he will know the implications of their handicap, understand their educational needs, and make necessary adjustments so that such children feel at home and secure in the class.

(iii) He should develop a positive attitude and show love and affection towards such children. The impact of the teacher's behaviour will be reflected in the behaviour of his peers.

(iv) He should arrange seats for them in the front row of the room, preferably on one side, so that they obtain a better view of both the teacher and the classmates.

(v) He should keep the auditory and visual distractors to a minimum. Although such distraction may not always be under the control of the teacher, excessive noises from the hall, other rooms, and outside should be eliminated, especially when he is talking. It should be remembered that environmental noises are also a problem for the child with a hearing aid, since all noises are amplified for him.

(vi) To optimize the child's opportunities to speech-read, the teacher should try to maintain a distance of about six feet between himself and the child. Standing too close can be a hindrance because it prevents the child from being able to observe situational cues.

(vii) The teacher should see that the hearing impaired child uses the hearing aid regularly and that the hearing aid is in perfect condition. If he notices any disorder or wrong use steps should be taken to rectify the defect and ensure correct use.

(viii) The teacher should speak naturally and follow other principles of speech reading and auditory training.

(ix) The teacher should attempt to standstill when talking, because excessive movement adds to the difficulty of speech reading.

(x) The teacher should be careful not to turn his back to the class and talk while writing on the black-board.

(xi) New vocabulary should be introduced both orally and in writing.

(xii) The teacher should encourage the child to ask questions when he is unsure of what is being told. When it is necessary to repeat something the teacher should try to rephrase the instruction. There are some words and phrases that are easier to lip read than others, and rephrasing increases the chances that the child will be exposed to words he can comprehend.

(xiii) The teacher should make every effort to use visual aids in the instructional process. The use of transparencies on an overhead projector (if possible) is a good way to do this. Simply writing instructions or new vocabulary items or important points on the black-board is another good method.

(xiv) The teacher should follow the teaching strategies and adapt the curriculum to the needs of the hearing-impaired child.

(xv) He should give opportunity to the hearing-impaired child to participate in various cocurricular activities in the class and the school depending on his abilities and interest.

(xvi) If the regular teacher has difficulty in managing or teaching the child in the class he should consult with the resource teacher and act accordingly.

5

Integrating the Visually Impaired

1. Who are the Visually Impaired Children?

It is an interesting phenomenon that visual impairment tends to evoke more awkwardness from us than any other disability. Why are we so uncomfortably aware of blindness? For one thing, blindness is visible. The blind person is usually not one who can easily weave himself into the fabric of a crowd. Unlike many other exceptional people he stands out. We often don't realize a person has impaired hearing until we talk to him. Likewise, the vast majority of mentally retarded individuals are indistinguishable from others on the basis of physical appearance. The visually impaired person, however, has a variety of symbols — cane, thick or darkened glasses, a guide dog etc.

Who are the visually impaired children? There are two prevailing ways of describing visual impairment — the legal definition and the educational definition. The legal definition is usually subscribed to by lay people and those in the medical profession. The educational definition is most often expoused by educators.

Legal/medical definition of blindness : The legal definition involves assessment of visual acquity and field of vision. It is used to determine whether or not an individual qualifies for legal benefits. The American Medical Association (AMA) proposed this definition in 1934. This definition is now accepted by the American Foundation for the Blind (AFB) and other Blind Associations in different countries.

"A legally blind person is said to be one (i) who has visual acquity of 20/200 or less in the better eye even with correction, (ii) or whose field of vision is so restricted that it subtends an angle of 20° or less in the better eye after correction." Visual acquity is the ability of the eye to see distant objects clearly which is determined with the help of Snellen Chart. The visual acquity of 20/200 refers to the fact that what a blind person can see at 20 feet a person with normal vision sees at 200 feet (normal visual acquity is 20/20). A simple method of testing visual acquity is to see whether an individual can count fingers at one metre distance, if he cannot, he is blind. Similarly the normal field of vision is 180 degrees in front of the eye. The field of vision of blind person is restricted to 20 degrees or less in front of the eye. Normally a man looking straight ahead can see the finger when it leaves the straight line stretching to the left and right of the eyes. When the peripheral vision of an individual is lost and his field of vision is restricted he cannot see the finger when it leaves the front of the eye and stretches to the left or right side of the eye. He is also called legally blind.

There are some individuals who are known as partially blind or partially sighted. The partially sighted are those whose visual acquity falls between 20/70 and 20/200 in the better eye even after correction. At times, the term 'low vision' and 'partially sighted' are used as synonyms. But it is a wrong usage. Low vision is defined in terms of reduction in the clarity of vision, whereas partially sightedness is defined in terms of the distance through the Snellen Chart for educational purpose. This distinction is very important. Educational programmes can differ for such cases.

Educational/functional definition of blindness : Many educators are distinterested in the legal or medical definition of blindness. Their argument is that visual acquity is not a very accurate predictor of how one will function or effectively use the remaining sight he has. A common misconception is that legally blind individuals have no sight. While a small percentage of the legally blind have absolutely no vision, the vast majority are able to see. Recognising the limitations of the legal definition of blindness and partial sightedness, many have favoured an educational definition. For educational purposes, "the blind are those who are so severely impaired that they must be taught to read by Braille, while the partially sighted can read print by using magnifying glasses or books with large print".

2. Identification and Placement of Visually Impaired Children

Identification of children who are born blind is almost always made by parents within the first year of life. Children with lesser visual impairments may not be singled out until elementary school when vision becomes important in the performance of school work.

One can take the help of a trained professional to identify the degree and nature of visual impairment. However, many children, especially those whose eyes may look normal by general appearance may not be identified for a long time. The teacher can identify children who might be having some sort of visual impairment with the help of the following check list developed by the NCERT, New Delhi. It must be remembered that no single behaviour signifies visual impairment.

Existence of more than one behaviour should ring the alarm for referral to proper specialists.

Identification Check List

Behaviour

(i) Rubs eyes excessively.
(ii) Covers one eye and tiltes the head forward.
(iii) Holds objects and books close to the eyes.
(iv) Asks other children when taking notes from the black-board.
(v) Blinks more frequently.
(vi) Squints eyelids together.
(vii) Bumps into people or objects.
(viii) Unable to participate in games requiring distance vision.
(ix) Excessive sensitivity to light.

Appearance

(i) Crossed eyes.
(ii) Red-rimmed, encrusted or swollen eyelids.
(iii) Inflamed or watery eyes.
(iv) Recurring styes.

Complaints

(i) Eyes itch, burn or feel scratchy.
(ii) Cannot see well.
(iii) Dizziness, headaches, or nausea following close eye work.
(iv) Blurred or double vision.

After identification of visual impairment by the teacher, such cases should be referred to specialists for medical assessment. If this is not possible or if it takes time then the resource teacher should conduct functional assessment of these children. Such children should be suitably placed in educational institutions so that they can receive the right type of education and training. There are basically four alternative educational placements for the visually impaired child.

(i) Placement in residential school.
(ii) Placement in special class in the regular school.
(iii) Placement in the regular classroom in the integrated setting with resource room support.
(iv) Placement in the regular classroom in integrated setting with itinerant teacher services.

Placement in residential school : Severely visually impaired children are usually placed in residential schools. Here the child is segregated from the home and his normal peers and spends the day and the night in the residential school. This kind of placement is, however, becoming much less popular. Professionals are recognising that the residential facility should usually be used as a last resort. In recent years, there has been a trend not to place blind children in residential institutions unless they have additional limiting handicaps, *e.g.* mental retardation, deafness, and so forth. The scheme of Integrated Education for Disabled Children sponsored by Government of India proposes to integrate blind children in regular classroom after they acquire braille reading and writing, mobility and orientation training etc. in residential institutions.

Placement in special class : A relatively popular placement is the special class placement. Within this framework, the child lives at home and spends all of the instructional time in a special class in the regular school. He is taught by teachers who are specially trained and qualified.

Placement in the regular classroom with resource room facility : The most effective and the least restrictive placement procedure is to place a blind child in the regular classroom with resource room facility. In this arrangement blind children are integrated with sighted children and are placed in the regular classroom. They spend half of the day with sighted children in the regular classroom and are taught by regular teachers. They are taken to the resource room for specialised instruction by the resource teacher for rest of the day. The child's education becomes the joint responsibility of the regular teachers and the resource teacher. This arrangement is effective only when sufficient number of blind children are enrolled in the regular school (minimum number is 8) to warrant for appointment of a resource teacher and construction of a resource room.

Placement in the regular classroom with itinerant teacher services : Placement in the regular classroom with provision of itinerant teacher services is recommended in cases where sufficient number of blind children are not available in any single school for appointment of a full time resource teacher. In such cases the resource teacher remains in charge of a cluster of schools. He moves from school to school and provides specialised instruction to blind children enrolled in these schools on scheduled days in consultation with the regular classroom teachers. This arrangement is very popular in rural and sparsely populated areas.

3. Characteristics of Visually Impaired Children

Language Development

(i) Many studies show that the language development of the

blind is unimpaired. The blind child is still able to hear language and may even be more motivated than the sighted child to use language because it is the major way in which he or she communicates with parents and peers.

(ii) Even though their language development is unimpaired it is different from the normal child's language. The language of the normal child is consistent with his sensory experiences. But the blind exhibits what is termed as verbalism or verbal unreality. Verbal unreality is defined as the blind individual's inappropriate reliance on words and phrases that are not consistent with his sensory experiences. Since the blind child explores his world primarily through the auditory, tactual and olfactory rather than the visual senses, it would seem that his language would reflect this fact. For example, most blind children perceive Indians as "red" or "brown" although they have no opportunity to see the colour of the skin. This is so because the blind are expected to appreciate things not as they themselves experience them, but as they are taught how others experience them. This verbalism is not inherent in the condition of blindness, rather it is taught to the individuals through the educational system.

Intellectual Ability

(i) The blind are not markedly lower in intelligence than the sighted. Children who have shown low IQ scores for a number of years in a sheltered environment suddenly make dramatic gains provided with adequate educational opportunities.

(ii) The conceptual or cognitive abilities of blind children are at least different, if not inferior to those of sighted children. Deficiencies in conceptual development of blind children are due to lack of appropriate learning experiences.

(iii) They have difficulty in comprehending space. Not able to see distances, blind individuals are at a distinct disadvantage in appreciating spatial concepts. Blind people apparently learn spatial concepts by the use of other senses than vision. The blind sometimes develop an appreciation of space by noting the time it takes to walk various distances and through touch and kinesthesis. Audition provides clues to the direction and distance of objects which make sound, but it gives no idea of the objects as such. Tactual and kinesthetic experiences require direct contact with or movement around objects. Thus, distant objects such as the heavenly bodies, clouds and the horizon, as well as very large objects such as mountains and other geographical units, or microscopic objects such as bacteria, cannot be perceived and must be conceived only by analogy and extrapolation from objects actually experienced.

(iv) The tactual sense is the primary way in which a variety of concepts are acquired by the blind child. There are two different kinds of tactual perception — synthetic touch and analytic touch. Synthetic touch refers to a person's tactual exploration of small objects which are small enough to be enveloped by one or both hands. Unfortunately most physical objects are too large for synthetic touch to be useful. For these physical objects analytic touch has to be used. Analytic touch involves the touching of various parts of an object and then mentally constructing these separate parts. Whereas the sighted person is able to perceive different objects or the parts of one object simultaneously, the blind person must perceive things successively. This necessity for perception in a successive manner restricts the blind child's ability to gain a conceptual understanding of his world.

(v) The visually impaired people develop an increased ability in attention because their reliance on other senses must be greater. They are very good at listening tasks. They score high on measures of creativity. Thus, even though they are greatly disadvantaged in terms to cognitive development they are able to compensate in many ways.

Mobility

Probably the most important ability for the successful adjustment of most visually impaired individuals is their mobility. Mobility refers to the skill of moving about in their environment. Mobility skills vary considerably in the visually impaired population. Some blind persons can move relatively easily through crowded city streets, some walk down a quiet street while some cannot move without a helper. The fact is that mobility would be better among those who have more residual vision than among those who have less. More significant is the fact that it is motivation to become mobile that makes the difference.

Academic achievement

Comparison of a visually impaired child's academic performance with that of a sighted child poses numerous problems. However, some gross generalizations can be made from the research that has been done.

(i) Both partially sighted and blind children are behind their sighted peers in terms of mental age.

(ii) The achievement of visually impaired children is not affected as greatly as is that of hearing impaired because hearing is evidently more important for school learning than is seeing.

Social and Work Adjustment

(i) Personality problems are not inherent in the condition of blindness. If maladjustment does occur in a blind individual, it is more than likely due to the fact that society has treated him differently. In other words it is society's reaction to the blind person that determines his adjustment or lack of it.

(ii) The visually impaired children are not well accepted by their peers. The more severely impaired are better accepted than the less severely handicapped. This is because people's sympathy tends to increase with the severity of a disability or because the moderately handicapped actually exhibit behaviours that elicit more negative reactions from others.

(iii) It is not necessarily the fact that blind persons tend to be dependent and helpless. The dependency and helplessness of blind persons are a result of society's attitude towards and expectations from the blind.

4. Care and Training of Visually Impaired

Every child whether normal, hearing impaired or visually impaired has a right to appropriate education and training. Every society must grant this right to the visually impaired so that they become useful members of the society.

The visually impaired children constitute a heterogenous group. Some are totally blind, some are partially sighted, some low vision and some one eyed. The care and training of such children must therefore match with the nature of their loss of vision. Care, training and education of such children must be the joint responsibility of parents, teachers and community members.

Most experts agree that, for the most part, the visually impaired should be educated in the same general way as the sighted following the same general principles. But some modifications in the teaching methodology may be needed.

(i) Use of remaining sight. The visually impaired children will have to rely on sensory modalities other than vision to acquire information. But they are to be encouraged to use their remaining sight or residual vision as much as possible. This is particularly advisable for partially sighted children.

(ii) Closed circuit television. A closed circuit television reader has been developed to aid partially sighted students in Western countries. A camera with a zoom lens photographs parts of a page of print and projects a magnified image on to the television screen. The student moves the book while reading so that the appropriate portion of the page is magnified. The size of the magnified print can be controlled.

(iii) Magnifying glasses and Hand magnifiers. The partially sighted children should be encouraged to read the print through magnifying glasses or hand magnifiers which present enlarged images of print.

(iv) Large print materials. The partially sighted children should be provided with large print materials. Large print books are simply volumes that contain print that is considerably larger than usual. The most common type recommended for such children is 18 point type or letters approximately one-eighth inch high. Such print reduces reading speed. However large print may be useful in case of reference books, dictionaries, mathematics and maps.

(v) Braille. Visually impaired children who cannot read regular print even with a magnifying device or large print materials should be trained to use Braille. Braille is a basic system of reading and writing for the blind. It consists of a six-dot cell that provides for sixtythree different characters. 26 combinations of dots are used for 26 letters of the alphabet. The remaining 37 combinations represent punctuation signs and contractions that allow for shortening or abbreviating words. In some ways braille is a system of shorthand since each word is not spelled out letter for letter. As a result blind children have difficulty with spelling because of the frequent abbreviations used in the Braille system. In addition to a Braille code for reading and writing there are codes for music, mathematics, computer sciences and chemistry.

Braille has many disadvantages. Books and periodicals printed in Braille are very bulky, expensive and take up a great deal of storage space. Moreover, Braille materials are not always available for all subjects and in all languages.

(vi) Talking calculator. Both the partially sighted and the blind may profit from a talking calculator. In the talking calculator, numerical entries are read aloud to the student through an earplug. Blind children may profit more from the talking calculator in learning Mathematics.

(vii) Tape recordings. Reading materials from both standard texts and books for leisure reading can be transcribed by the teacher and presented to the blind who usually profit from audio-aural cues more than visual cues. The use of tape recording is gaining in popularity as a method of teaching language, history, geography, science etc. The blind can cover the same material much more quickly.

The whole gamut of the curriculum for children in school is centred around two significant aspects — the opportunity and the experience. Often children are provided with opportunities, but the mere provision of opportunities does not mean the acquisition of experience.

Sighted children have an edge over blind children in the acquisition of knowledge through experience. Sighted children acquire rich experiences in a natural way. They learn the experience as a 'whole'. But the learning of blind children is in 'pieces' of information. There is thus a need for different approaches to the curriculum for blind children.

(viii) General Curriculum with Modified Experiences. Many experts agree that blind children should be educated in the same general way, following the same general principles and along with sighted children in the regular schools or in integrated setting. The curriculum for blind children should be more like that of the sighted children. Most information is received by the visually handicapped child through touch and hearing. Hence, these experiences must be planned to facilitate the acquisition of near normal experience acquired by sighted children through vision. Multisensory experiences are to be provided to blind children to acquire near-normal experiences.

The visual experience should be converted into non-visual experience for concept development of blind children. For this purpose the teacher should follow the following steps :

- — Give duplicate experiences as far as practicable,
- — Modify the experiences in terms of content, method of display, type of materials used and response expectations from the child.
- — Substitute the lesson to a different lesson which as closely as possible approximates that presented to the sighted children.
- — Omit a lesson sometimes if the former three steps are not possible.

(ix) The Plus Curriculum. The plus curriculum is always recommended for blind children. The plus curriculum is not something extra as the name may appear to indicate. It is comprensatory. It contains skills and competencies which, if developed early, result in the learning of the general curriculum meant for sighted children. The special areas of the plus curriculum are as follows :

— Braille
— Orientation and Mobility
— Daily living skills
— Sensory training
— Social skills
— Use of equipment like braillers and abacus.

(x) Cocurricular Activities. Visually impaired children should be given the opportunity for participation in cocurricular activities in the school. Keeping in view their visual impairment and their possibilities in performing cocurricular activities the following activities are recommended for them.

Singing, playing instruments, debating, composing poems (The visually impaired children may take part in all these activities with sighted children).

Games and sports with provision of auditory cues for visually impaired child (for examples, a bell ball can replace the ordinary ball used by sighted children in football match).

Since visually impaired children demonstrate slow pace of performance in cocurricular activities, in no case should they be compared with sighted children. The approach in this case should be purely on an individual basis.

5. Role of the Teacher

Managing the Visually Impaired

Visually impaired children are now attending regular classes in increasing number. Expecting few modifications they are pursuing the same general curriculum in regular schools. The resource teacher is there to provide resource room instruction to the visually impaired children. But as we all know education of handicapped children is the joint responsibility of the resource teacher and the regular teachers. In fact education of handicapped children is ultimately the responsibility of the regular teachers. The resource teacher is a support teacher. Regular teachers should therefore know how to handle such children.

(i) The visually impaired child has the same right to education as the sighted children. But very often blind children are denied the opportunity to receive education in general schools. In fact, if a blind child has completed his preparation in a special school there is no point why he should not be enrolled in a general school.

(ii) While planning to provide education to visually impaired children in the regular classroom the regular teacher should contact and consult with the resource teacher. The resource teacher who is a specialist in the methodology of special education can guide the regular teacher in the teaching-learning process.

(iii) The regular teacher should ask the visually impaired child to care for his own materials as part of his effort to foster a sense of independence.

(iv) He may ask a sighted child in the class to act at times as a guide as long as the visually disabled pupil does not become too dependent upon him.

(v) The blind child should be treated in the same way as his sighted peers. The same experiences should be provided to both the sighted and the visually impaired children.

(vi) The regular teacher should encourage healthy interaction between the visually impaired and the sighted children.

(vii) Visually impaired children should be encouraged by the regular teacher to participate in as many activities of the school as possible. If it is not possible for the visually impaired child to join with the rest of the class in some activity the regular teacher should plan alternate activities for him.

(viii) The regular teacher should give the same kinds of special tasks to the visually impaired that are given to other children.

(ix) The regular teacher should ensure a proper physical environment in the classroom for the partially sighted children. Adequate illumination is a must. The seating arrangement is also very important. The child should be seated so that he can best see the chalkboard and other materials. Glossy pictures should be avoided. Visual materials should be free from distracting background materials. The teacher should write on the chalkboard in large and clear letters. In addition, because of the great amount of visual attention the child must maintain frequent rest periods as may be necessary.

(x) While teaching, most teachers use many non-verbal signs/cues which are inappropriate for the visually impaired. It is therefore important for the teacher to verbalise his intents to the visually impaired child.

(xi) Initially the direction, location and the distance of various objects, rooms and other essential things should be made clear to the visually impaired child.

(xii) The important thing in teaching visually impaired children is to help them to learn the maximum possible while at the same time encouraging their sense of independence and accomplishment. The purpose of assimilating them into the regular classroom is to help them learn to function as effectively as possible in the world and the teachers role in this regard is a vital and challenging one.

6

Integrating the Mentally Retarded

1. Concept of Mental Retardation

We have people amongst us, some who are rich and others who are poor, some who are tall and some others who are short and some are fair and some others who are dark. Some people are strong and some others are weak. Similarly we have people with different mental abilities — average, more than average, and less than average. People with less than average mental ability are called mentally retarded. Such people have difficulty in changing their way of functioning appropriate to the various situations in every day life. The term 'mental retardation', 'mental deficiency', 'mental handicap', and 'mental subnormality' refer to the same condition. The terms used in the past such as amentia, idiocy, feeble minded, moron, imbecile, and oligophrenia are now obsolete.

There are many definitions of mental retardation. The most comprehensive among them is the one given by the American Association on Mental Retardation (AAMR). The definition as given in 1983 is :

"Mental Retardation refers to *significantly sub-average general intellectual functioning*, resulting in or associated with concurrent impairments in *adaptive behaviour*, and manifested during the *developmental period*."

Let us define the key terms in the definition cited above :

(i) '*General Intellectual Functioning*' is defined as the results obtained by the administration of standardized general intelligence tests developed for the purpose, and adapted to the conditions of the region/country.

(ii) '*Significantly Subaverage*' is defined as IQ of 70 or below on standardized measures of intelligence. The upper limit is intended as a guideline; it could be extended to 75 or more, depending upon the reliability of intelligence test used.

(iii) '*Adaptive Behaviour*' is defined as the degree with which the individual meets the standards of personal independence and social responsibility expected of his age and cultural group. The expectations of adaptive behaviour may be reflected in the following areas :

— During infancy and early childhood in
  Sensory and motor skill development.
  Communication skills (including speech and language).
  Self help skills.
  Socialization.

— During childhood and adolescence in
  Application of basic academic skills to daily life activities.
  Application of appropriate reasoning and judgement in the mastery of the environment.
  Social skills.

— During late adolescence and adult life in
  Vocational and social responsibilities and performances.

(iv) '*Developmental Period*' is defined as the period of time between conception and the 18th birthday.

Before labelling a person as mentally retarded especially in the mild category, certain factors have to be considered. Members belonging to low socio-economic groups and certain cultures may score low on standard tests of intelligence and thus may be labelled as mentally retarded. However, they will be functioning within normal limits according to their culture's criteria. Therefore, one must be cautious before labelling a person as mentally retarded.

Adaptive behaviour is given much more emphasis in determining whether or not a person is retarded. Thus, a child can score low on a test of intelligence but have adaptive skills. A child may do poorly in school but still be able to cope with the rural life, with peers, and after school job. Some children may function in the retarded range while they are in school for six hours of the day but behave normally once they return to the home community for the rest eighteen hours.

A child should not be labelled as mentally retarded simply because he scores low on intelligence test or because he has deficits in adaptive behaviour. A child is to be regarded as mentally retarded only when all the three conditions are noticed in him :

(i) Significantly subaverage intellectual functioning;
(ii) Deficits in adaptive behaviour and
(iii) The first two conditions are observed during the developmental period.

Mental retardation and mental illness. Mental Retardation is not the same as mental illness. Mental retardation is a condition. It cannot be cured. But persons suffering from mental illness can be helped to learn many things. One of the major features of mental retardation is delayed development. Some mentally retarded persons have external characteristics such as —

a small head,
big or small and slanting eyes,
squint,
a thick tongue,
the drooling of saliva,
irregular teeth,
short and fat limbs and
flat feet.

On the other hand people suffering from mental illness have normal development of physical and mental abilities. Mental illness can be cured with medical and psychiatric help. Some of the external symptoms of mental illness are :

behaving in a strange manner,
becoming moody and withdrawn,
having suicidal tendencies,
seeing and hearing things which others do not see and hear, suspecting others abnormally and
becoming unusually cheerful and boastful.

Classification of MR. There are mainly three methods of classification of mental retardation. They are medical, psychological and educational. The psychological and educational classifications are more commonly and widely used than the medical classification. The medical classification is based on the cause of retardation. The psychological classification is based on the severity of retardation. The psychological classification was originally recommended by the American Association of Mental Deficiency and is now used in the special schools in India. The educational classification which was originally recommended by American educators has also been recommended by the NCERT, New Delhi for use in IED schools. The educational classification is based on the educational needs and educability of retarded persons.

The psychological classification system uses the terms mild, moderate, severe, and profound depending on the severity of retardation. The intellectual level in terms of IQ scores of these four groups of MR children is presented below :

Mild Retardation	IQ 55 to 70
Moderate Retardation	IQ 40 to 54
Severe Retardation	IQ 25 to 39
Profound Retardation	IQ below 25

The Educational classification system uses the term educable, trainable and custodial depending on the educational needs of retarded children. The IQ ranges of educable mentally retarded (EMR), trainable mentally retarded (TMR) and the custodial mentally retarded (CMR) are given below :

Educable Mentally Retarded (EMR)	IQ 50 to 75
Trainable Mentally Retarded (TMR)	IQ 25 to 50
Custodial Mentally Retarded (CMR)	IQ below 25

The educable mentally retarded children are those who can be taught the basic academic subjects. The trainable mentally retarded are those children who can be taught functional academics with emphasis on self-help and vocational skills. The custodial mentally retarded are those children who require constant and special care specially in a residential institution. The educable mentally retarded children, the mildly retarded and some moderately retarded children having IQ 50 and above can be integrated in the general schools.

Two Systems of Classification of MR children

System	IQ Ranges: 100 95 90 85 80 75 70 65 60 55 50 45 40 35 30 25 20 15 10 5			
Psychological	Mild	Moderate	Severe	Profound
Educational	Educable	Trainable		Custodial

2. Identification and Placement of MR Children

(a) *Identification by Parents* : Growth and development of children follow a pattern. Every child passes through certain stages at particular time in his life. These stages are called milestones of development. It is important to know the normal milestones of development as it helps in identifying children who have delayed development. Some of the common milestones of development and the approximate age of their attainment relevant to Indian situations are given in Appendix 1. It should be kept in mind that some children may skip few of the stage.

From Appendix 1 you can see how a normal child develops. Early identification of mental retardation is made by seeing how much a child is delayed on the milestones of development. Identification of mental retardation is done by using certain questionnaires or checklists called screening schedules. Three screening schedules are given in Appendix 1. The first is for the children below 3 years of age. The second for those between 3 — 6 years of age. The third is for those aged 7 years and above. In the description of normal milestones of development the mean age of attainment alone is given. However, the age range has to be taken into consideration while screening for developmental delays. Hence, the age range is given in the Screening Schedule 1.

(b) *Identification by Teachers* : The screening schedules are very useful in identification of MR children by the parents. The teachers, psychologists and multi-rehabilitation workers can also identify MR children before they come to the primary school for education with the help of these schedules. But there are a large number of mildly and moderately retarded children who are already in schools. If they remain unidentified and if their educational and other special needs are not met they will experience failure and dropout from the school. The teachers can identify MR children who are already in school by observing certain behavioural characteristics. The following identification checklist is recommended by the NCERT, New Delhi for identification of MR children who are already in school :

Identification Checklist for MR Children

— Displays poor academic achievements constantly.

— Relies too much on presentation of concrete objects.

— Has a short attention span.

— Displays short term memory.

— Has a poor self-image.

— Lacks self-confidence.

— Has restricted communication.

— Seeks repetition and practice.

— Does not take any initiative in group activities.

— Often inattentive and distracted.

— Needs immediate reward.

— Displays fear of failure.

— Has poor muscular coordination.
— Faces difficulty in doing things for himself.
— Has problem in understanding instructions.
— Is unable to sit in one place for more than a few minutes.
— Exhibits restless activities like tapping, pulling and so on.
— Has problems in speech.
— Is hyperactive.

After identifying a child with MR he should be referred to specially trained experts for medical and psychological assessment and diagnosis. Until that is done the resource teacher may conduct functional assessment to arrive at a tentative picture of the current level of functioning of the child and his educational needs.

Placement of MR children ; After medical and psychological assessment, the MR child should be placed in a suitable environment/institution for proper care and training. Usually the following kinds of placement are recommended for MR children. The appropriate placement depends upon the degree of retardation.

(i) Placement in Regular Classes.
(ii) Placement in Resource Room.
(iii) Placement in Special Classes.
(iv) Placement in Special Schools.
(v) Placement in Residential Institutions.
(vi) Placement in Group Home.
(vii) Placement in Activity Centres.

Mildly retarded children are to be placed in the regular classes and resource rooms in IED schools. Moderately retarded children are usually placed in special classes; sheltered workshops for older individuals are also common in various countries. At the preschool level, moderately retarded children are sometimes placed in special day schools. Placement in residential institution is sometimes recommended for moderately retarded children when other types of handicap such as deafness are present and are severe and when community placement is not available or when the family situation is undesirable. Severely and profoundly retarded children are usually placed in residential institutions.

A placement programme growing in popularity is the group home. In group home arrangement many formerly institutionalised individuals are placed in relatively small groups (three to ten people) in houses under the direction of employed house parents. The level of retardation of individuals in these homes ranges from mild to severe. Group homes accommodate children, adolescents or adults. But every group home focuses upon a specific age range. Placement in group home can either be a permanent arrangement or a temporary living arrangement depending upon the level of retardation and the training required. For many parents of retarded individuals, the group home provides a positive and less stigmatised alternative to institutional placement.

Another type of arrangement that is becoming more popular is the activity centre suitable for severely and profoundly retarded individuals. The activity centre is a place where parents can take their children for a portion of the day for a variety of activities related to recreation and crafts. The basic purpose is socialization and not formal training.

3. Characteristics of MR Children

What are the mentally retarded people like? The mentally retarded people have many things in common with the normal people. But there are also characteristics which are different. The characteristics of MR children are mentioned differently in different literature by various authorities. Some describe the characteristics which are generally noticed in MR children and then go on to say that all MR children may not display all the characteristics. Their argument is that there is a great deal of variability in the behaviour of the retarded, and each MR child must be considered as a unique and separate person. Some authorities describe the characteristics according to the severity of retardation while some others mention the characteristics not according to the degree of disability but in terms of their educability. From whatever angle one may consider, the characteristics of MR children are as follows :

(1) General Characteristics of MR Children

(i) *Slow reaction* : They respond slowly to what others say and to what happens in their surroundings. Sometimes they do not respond at all.

(ii) *Absence of clarity* : They cannot express clearly their thoughts, needs and feelings

(iii) *Inability to learn fast* : They cannot learn anything new and different as easily as others. They are slow in learning.

(iv) *Inability to understand quickly* : They cannot understand easily what they see, hear, touch, smell or taste.

(v) *Inability to decide* : They cannot take even small decisions. They do not know what to do, say and so on.

(vi) *Lack of concentration* : Some mentally retarded children cannot give continuous attention to one person or one activity. Some of them have difficulty in changing from one activity to another.

(vii) *Short temper* : Some find it difficult to control their feelings. They may throw things all over, injure themselves or others.

(viii) *Inability to remember* : Some can remember only for a short time of what they are told. Sometimes they do not remember at all.

(ix) *Lack of coordination* : Some have difficulty in sucking, chewing or eating, use of hands or moving from place to place.

(x) *Delay in development* : The mentally retarded children have delayed development. Three screening schedules are given in Appendix-1. If the child is found to be delayed in development as per the responses in the screening schedule, mental retardation is suspected.

(2) Specific Characteristics of EMR, TMR and CMR Children

Educable Mentally Retarded (EMR). The EMR children have IQ 50 to 75. They have normal appearance and remain unidentified until late teens. They function at an intellectual level generally limited to learning the most basic school subjects, skills such as reading, spelling, writing and numerical calculation. They are expected to learn up to the seventh standard. They can communicate effectively in everyday conversation, enjoy friendship and group social activities. They can travel with ease in their home town or locality. During adulthood, they are able to live independently, marry or have children. They can hold skilled or semi-skilled jobs. But at times they may need assistance in doing their job. They can be educated in regular classrooms.

Trainable Mentally Retarded (TMR). The TMR children have IQ 25 to 50. They are expected to have physical or sensory impairments and many tend to look different in terms of facial features and physical characteristics. They function at a level where formal academic learning is quite limited. They can learn to feed, toilet and dress self adequately. They can carry on rudimentary conversation, and do simple house hold work. But they need training in self care activities, language development and rudimentary academic skills. They are usually placed in special classes or special schools.

Custodial Mentally Retarded (CMR). The CMR children have IQ below 25. They are so much retarded in intellectual functioning and adaptive behaviour that they remain totally dependent on others for their existence. It is because of their severe retardation that they are institutionalised early in life. Their speech and toilet habits remain at a primitive level. Behaviour modification and environmental stimulation techniques are usually recommended for their training.

4. Care and Training of Educable Mentally Retarded Children

The centrally sponsored scheme of IED envisages for early identification, assessment and education of mildly retarded and educable mentally retarded children in general schools. Most of these children are already in the schools unidentified. Unless EMR children are identified early and unless adequate measures are taken for their care, training and education they will experience failure and later drop out from the school before completing the basic education. They will not only remain as burdens for the society but universalisation of elementary education will not be successful. EMR children, like any other normal children, have the same fundamental rights to exist, training, education and work and this calls for greater public understanding and awareness about the problems and special needs of such children. Care, training and education of such children are not the sole responsibilities of teachers. Parents and the community have also equal responsibilities in the care and training of such children.

Parents' responsibility : Care and training of EMR children should start in the family.

(i) Experienced mothers, the grandmother and other old women in the family are familiar with normal milestones of development. If a child is found to have delayed development and if abnormalities are noticed in his physical and intellectual developments and if deficiencies are noticed in his adaptive behaviour he should be referred to paedriaticians and child psychologists for diagnosis and treatment.

(ii) Parents should not feel dejected and disappointed about the condition of their children. They should not loose patience but instead should take all possible steps to prevent further damage through proper care and training as per the advice of doctors, psychologists and teachers.

(iii) Home-based training is most effective and provides the foundation for later learning in the school. Parents and particularly the mother should create conditions and teach the child daily living skills, social skills, communication skills and pre-academic skills during the first few years under reinforced practice and through enjoyable activities. Listening skills, attending skills, naming objects, manipulating objects, awareness of self, responding to and greeting others, conversation, reading pictures, music, play, games and story telling should be emphasized in the home-based training programme.

Specific Characteristics of MR Children at Different Severity Levels/Ages

Severity level/ Description	Mild	Moderate	Severe	Profound
Pre-schools 0 — 5 years	Can develop social and communication skills; minimal retardation in sensori motor areas; often not distinguished from normal until late age.	Can talk or learn to communicate; poor social awareness; fair motor development; profits from training in self help; can be managed with moderate supervision.	Poor motor development; speech minimal; generally unable to profit from taraining in self-help; little or no communication skills.	Gross retardation; minimal capacity for functioning in sensori motor areas; needs nursing care.
School age 6 — 20 years Training and Education	Can learn academic skills upto approximately 6th grade level by late teens; can be guided towards social confirmity.	Can profit from training in social and occupational skills; unlikely to progress beyond 2nd grade level in academic subject; may learn to travel alone in familiar places.	Can talk or learn to communicate; can be trained in elementary health habits; profits from systematic habit training.	Some motor development present; may respond to minimal or limited training in self-help.

(*Contd.*)

Severity level/ Description	Mild	Moderate	Severe	Profound
Adult 21 and over Social and Vocational Adequacy	Can usually achieve social and vocational skills adequate to minimum self-support but needs assistance when under unusual social or economic stress.	May achieve self-maintenance in unskilled or semi-skilled work under sheltered conditions; needs supervision and guidance when under mild social or economic stress.	May contribute partially to self-maintenance under complete supervision; can develop self protection skills to a minimal useful level in controlled environment.	Some motor and speeh development; may achieve very limited self-care; needs nursing care.

Pre-School Education : Educable mentally retarded children in the age group of 3 to 6 years should be given pre-school education. During this period emphasis should be on developing readiness skills which are prerequisites for later learning of academics. Readiness skills are also recommended for normal youngsters. But pre-school classes for the mildly retarded child should start at a lower level and the training of these skills may take as long as two or three years rather than one year. Readiness skills include the ability to :

(i) Sit still and attend to the teacher.

(ii) Discriminate auditory and visual stimuli.

(iii) Follow directions.

(iv) Develop language.

(v) Increase gross and fine motor coordination (*e.g.* holding a pencil, cutting with a pair of scissors)

(vi) Develop self-help skills (*e.g.* tying shoes, buttoning and unbuttoning, zipping and unzipping, toileting).

(vii) Interact with peers in group situations. In short pre-school education should be a continuation of home-based training with re-emphasis on teaching sensori-motor skills, communication skills, social skills, daily living or self-help skills and pre-academic skills. The nature of training in pre-school classes depends on the degree of retardation, special needs and deficiencies in the child and the quality of home training received by the child.

Education in general school

(i) EMR children should receive education in common with others in general schools. Educational programme for the EMR children should aim at development of (a) Academic skills, (b) Social competence, (c) Personal adjustment, and (d) Occupational adequacy.

(ii) Depending upon the nature of retardation they may be educated in the regular classroom or regular classroom with part time instruction in the resource room or special class in the regular school.

(iii) The curriculum at the primary stage should be an extension of that of pre-school education. The curriculum for EMR children should be oriented towards providing readiness skills, language development, concept formation, socially adaptive behaviours and teaching basics of reading, mathematics and handwriting. Teaching of tool subjects such as reading, arithmetic, handwriting, oral language should be very simple and interesting and of the standard expected of normal kindergarten-age children.

(iv) If some retarded children are in need of special class instruction the following principles should be followed :

— The younger the children, the smaller the class.

— The more heterogenous the group, the smaller the class.

— Special class should always be organised within the regular primary school.

— Special class instruction should be given by the resource teacher or the itinerant teacher only.

— Adequate diagnosis should be made before they are placed in the special class.

— The resource teacher should have considerable freedom in adapting the curriculum to the needs of individual children.

(v) Whether the retarded child is educated in the regular classroom or resource room, instruction should be systematic and sequential in nature.

(vi) As the child makes progress in the class less and less emphasis should be placed on readiness skills and more and more emphasis should be given on academic skills and the basic tool subjects such as reading, writing and arithmetic.

(vii) Emphasis should be gradually placed on work-habits, vocational training, and family life education as the child makes progress from primary education to the secondary education. This should be particularly emphasized for older retarded students.

Vocational training should actually pass through five phases, such as, vocational exploration, vocational evaluation, vocational training, vocational placement and follow up. In the phase of vocational exploration, the MER student is familiarized with the nature of various occupations and their skill requirements. In the second phase the retarded student is exposed to experiences with different job skills in order to determine the vocational abilities and preferences of the student. In the third phase emphasis is given on developing job skills and on preparing the student for a range of occupations. This is the stage of on-the-job experiences. The fourth stage consists of locating a job for the student and placing him in the job. The last stage entails counselling and further training or replacement.

The EMR students should also be given knowledge about marriage, family life, child rearing, responsible parenthood, relationship and responsibilities of various members in the family etc. so that such students, when they grow up, will behave rationally and in a responsible way in relation to various aspects of marriage and family life. They should also be educated about civic rights and responsible citizenship.

5. Role of the Teacher

A large number of mildly and some moderately retarded children do enter the regular primary schools. They remain unidentified and unnoticed for some years until their problems become so serious that they experience failure and frustration and later drop-out from the school. This calls for early identification, diagnosis and assessment and making instruction systematic and sensitive. The regular classroom teacher has to play a significant role in teaching such children in the regular classroom.

(i) The regular teacher should be familiar with the behavioural characteristics of MR children for purpose of identifying and referring them to the psychologist for assessment.

(ii) He should develop a positive and optimistic view about the educability of such children.

(iii) He should avoid as far as possible labelling the child, passing on damaging remarks and also see that the non-retarded peers behave in a positive way with the child.

(iv) He should create favourable conditions in his class and the school for social and academic integration of EMR children.

(v) He should constantly attempt to sequence learning tasks. Relatively complex units should be broken down into a hierarchy of sub-units and attempt should be made to teach one sub-unit at a time, help children to learn the sub unit, and then to proceed to the next sub-unit.

(vi) The teacher should encourage retarded children to make use of verbal mediation in learning the tool subjects. The retarded child should rehearse verbally what he is to learn and remember. Verbal mediation is a very useful learning strategy for learning concepts and problem-solving.

(vii) Retarded children do not know how to learn different subjects. Learning to learn is a useful technique for retarded children. The retarded child should be told verbally and exposed to models and tutoring by non-disabled peers for learning how to learn.

(viii) Many retarded children learn best by drill and repetition. Thus the teacher should give emphasis on drill and repetition in teaching language items and arithmetic skills.

(ix) Retarded children learn best through concrete experiences, play-way method, audio-visual aids and action-oriented teaching, etc. The regular teacher should, therefore, make use of concrete objects, story-telling, dramatization, music, dance, play situations, multisensory approach, coloured pictures, picture cards, word cards and toy materials in the teaching-learning situations.

(x) Many retarded individuals may be lacking in motivation. The regular teacher should look for ways to increase the motivation of such children. Interesting pictures and stories and novelty can increase motivation. However, progress should be from known to unknown, familiar to new experiences.

(xi) The retarded child should be given success experiences in learning tool subjects and social behaviours. Each experience of a retarded child should be followed by a consistent programme of reinforcement and feedback. Praise, recognition, reward, positive remarks, love and affection can have stimulating effects on the child in learning various skills.

(xii) The retarded child should be given opportunity to participate in classroom activities and cocurricular activities in the school. Such children can participate in drawing, painting, games and sports, music, songs and drama, gardening, beautification of school campus, celebrations and observations, etc.

(xiii) Continuous assessment should be made by the regular teacher about the child's level of functioning. This assessment may be either formal or informal.

(xiv) The regular teacher should seek the advice of the resource teacher whenever he has difficulty with the child's learning and behaviour. The resource teacher who is a consultant in the methodology of teaching the retarded children can help the regular teacher in teaching and behaviour modification techniques.

7

Integrating the Learning Disabled

1. What is Learning Disability?

There are a substantial number of children who have problems in learning specific subjects. Usually learning problems may occur due to any one or a combination of the following factors :

Low level of intelligence

Mental retardation

Visual impairment

Motor handicaps

Economic difficulties

Cultural disadvantage

Poor instruction, etc.

Learning problems caused by the above mentioned factors are not considered to be learning disability. For example, a mentally retarded child has learning problems in all school subjects. The learning problems of a mentally retarded child are not caused by learning disability but low level of intelligence. Similarly learning problems of a blind child are due to his visual impairment and this is not learning disability.

The Concept

Learning disability refers to learning problems which manifest in an imperfect ability to listen, think, speak, read, write or do mathematical calculations which are not primarily due to visual impairment, hearing impairment, motor handicap, mental retardation, environmental or economic disadvantages, but due to a disorder in the psychological process involved in understanding or in using language.

Kirk (1962) says : "Learning disability refers to a retardation, disorder, or delayed development in one or more of the processes of speech, language, reading, spelling, writing or arithmetic resulting from a possible cerebral dysfunction and/or emotional or behavioural disturbance and not from mental retardation, sensory deprivation, cultural or instructional factors."

The definition of learning disability adopted by National Advisory Committee on Handicapped Children (USA, 1968) is given as under :

"Children with specific learning disabilities exhibit a disorder in one or more of the basic psychological processes involved in understanding or using spoken or written language. These may be manifested in disorders of listening, thinking, talking, reading, writing, spelling or arithmetic. They include conditions which have been referred to as perceptual handicaps, dyslexia, development aphasia, etc. They do not include learning problems which are due primarily to visual, hearing, motor handicaps, mental retardation, emotional disturbances, or environmental disadvantages."

The National Joint Committee of Learning Disabilities (USA, 1981) gave the following definition of learning disability which is unanimously accepted at international level :

"Learning disability is a generic term that refers to a heterogenous group of disorders manifested by significant difficulties in the acquisition and use of listening, speaking, reading, writing, reasoning or mathematical abilities. These disorders are intrinsic to the individual and presumed to be due to central nervous system dysfunction. Even though learning disability may occur concomitantly with other handicapping conditions (*e.g.*, sensory impairment, mental retardation, social and emotional disturbance) or environmental influences (*e.g.*, cultural differences, insufficient/inappropriate instruction, psychogenic factors) it is not the direct result of these conditions or influences."

The term learning disability refers to conditions which were previously called brain injury, minimal brain dysfunction, sensory aphasia (the loss of the power to understand spoken words, signs, gestures or print), expressive aphasia (the loss of the ability to speak), alexia or word blindness (the loss of the ability to read — a mild degree of alexia is called dyslexia), acalculia (the loss of arithmetical ability — at a lower level it is called dyscalculia) — agraphia (the inability to learn to write — a mild degree of agraphia is called dysgraphia).

Degree of Disability : In terms of degree, learning disability may be of two types — mild LD and severe LD. The mild learning disabled can be educated in regular schools. Such children are to be found in regular schools. They are, however, difficult to identify at the initial stages. They face problems in learning basic academic skills. Their problem may occur in one or more areas of learning skill in a relatively mild degree. The severe learning disabled include those who manifest an inability to master basic academic skills (reading, writing etc.). Their problems may be due to brain dysfunction or environmental deprivation. It is difficult to integrate such children in regular schools. Whatever may be the degree of disability there is always a discrepancy between achievement and ability of such children. This is the basic problem that they face.

The LD and MR Children : The LD children are very often confused and misunderstood as MR children. In reality, LD children are not mentally retarded. Both LD and MR children have problems in learning academic subjects. They have their own learning styles. The achievement level of MR children may match with their intellectual functioning. Usually such children experience failure in all aspects of life and in all school subjects. Such children may learn up to the seventh standard. But in case of LD children, there is always a discrepancy between their level of intelligence (what one can do) and their actual level of achievement (what one does at present). They have problems in specific areas such as reading, speaking, writing, spelling, etc. With appropriate educational intervention LD children can rise to a level which seems unbelievable at present.

The LD, Backward Children, and Slow Learners : The LD children are not the same as backward children and slow learners. The problems of backward children or slow learners may be due to low intelligence, environmental, cultural, or social disadvantages, psychological and emotional hazards, or defective instruction. But the problems of learning disabled children are not primarily caused due to these factors. A backward child or a slow learner may perform poorly in all academic areas. But a learning disabled child has difficulty only in a specific academic area such as reading, writing, or arithmetic. The factors which cause slow learning or backwardness in learning are known to everybody. But the causes of learning disability are still a mystery.

Types of Learning Disability. Learning disability may occur in various forms such as reading disability, writing disability, communication and comprehension disability, numerical disability, etc.

Reading Disability : Children suffering from reading disability are unable to read. There are two forms of this disability. In a mild form the affected person has difficulty in reading, but in severe cases of the impairment there is a total loss of the ability to read. This is sometimes also known as 'Word Blindness'. Children with the mild form of the disability are already in the general classroom. If identified early, proper help can be given and integration with their normal peers is also easier. The severely affected child will need intensive remedial exercises.

Writing Disability : The affected children are not able to write spontaneously. There are two forms of this impairment — the mild and severe. Children affected by the mild form have difficulty in learning to write legibly. They study in general schools. Their problems can be corrected if identified early and provided timely help. Those affected by the severe type of impairment can copy writing without distoration but they cannot write spontaneously. They are identified by their inability to learn to write. The severely affected children need remedial exercises and are thus hard to integrate in the academic areas.

Problems in Comprehending Communication : Children with this disability have a problem in communication through writing, speaking, or reading. Those affected by the mild form of this impairment have difficulty in understanding both the spoken and written words. The child finds it difficult to understand even signs and gestures. These children can be integrated if corrective measures are given in time. Otherwise, linguistic problems of articulation and fluency may develop. The severely affected child is unable to understand speech and written material, nor can he learn to speak, read and write. He is unable to communicate even through signs and gestures. Such children are difficult cases for integration. They need intensive remedial exercises.

Problems of Numerical Ability : The affected child has problems in calculations, even simple arithmetic, because of an inability to manipulate number relationships. Numerical inability is again of two kinds — mild and severe. Numerical problems seem difficult even if they are very simple for a normal child to do. Children with the mild form of this disability may already be studying in the general classroom. They are not easily identified at pre-primary levels. The disability becomes obvious when they start learning numbers and simple addition and substraction. If identified early and with appropriate correction, they can study in the regular classes. If the problem is severe, the child will not be able to learn number symbols and their relationships. This is also termed as loss of arithmetic ability. The severe cases are difficult for integration and will require intensive remedial exercises.

2. Identification and Placement of LD Children

The LD children are usually identified by the following methods and techniques :

(i) Interview with children and their parents.

(ii) Observation by teachers.

(iii) Informal testing by teachers.

(iv) Formal testing by the assessment team.

Tests commonly used for identification purposes include intelligence tests, achievement tests and diagnostic tests. The classroom teacher can identify such children by observing their behavioural characteristics consistently for a period of time. Observation by a team of teachers is more useful in identifying such children. The following checklist is recommended by NCERT, New Delhi for identification of LD children.

Identification Checklist for the LD children

— Has difficulty in telling the time, remembering the order of days, months and seasons and mathematical tables.

— Finds it difficult to organize his work and is often late in submitting his class-work.

— Seems dull and slow in responding to others.

— Cannot correctly recall oral instructions when asked to repeat them.

— Does not seem to listen to or understand instructions given at home or in the classroom (asks for repetition).

— Shows excessive inconsistency in the quality of performance; from time to time; seems to be bright in many ways, but still does poorly in school.

— Gets easily distracted even by a slight disturbance.

— Confuses between left and right.

— Gets so excited that he cannot sit still in the classroom even for a short period.

— While reading, misses outlines or reads them twice.

— Finds difficulty in synthesising a word after spelling its component letters : Example : says b/e/g but cannot say beg, or may say bed instead.

— Makes wild guesses at words whether they make sense or not (for example, 'huge' for 'hurt', 'turned' for 'trainer').

— Reads word backwards (for example 'on' for 'no', 'saw' for 'was').

— Puts letters in the wrong order (reading 'felt' as 'left', 'act' as 'cat').

— Shortens words ('sunly' for 'suddenly', 'member' for 'remember').

— Misreads words which look similar ('help' for 'held', 'house' for 'horse').

— Has difficulty in recollecting words automatically and correct sentences.

— Misreads number ('6' as '9', '3' as '8') writes letters in the wrong order (time for 'item').

— Mirror writes (ram for mar).
— Reverses letter ('b' as 'd', 'p' as 'q').
— Mirror writes (6 as '9', 'q' as 'p').
— Omits letters ('limp' as 'lip', 'went' as 'wet').
— Adds letters ('want' as 'what', 'what' as 'whart').
— Does not write the appropriate letters when given the sound.
— Does not pick out letter of the alphabet when the name of the letter is called out.
— Does not match the letters when asked to.
— Difficulty in academic subjects. Sometimes the student is deficient in only one subject or a combination of subjects.

After identifying LD children by using the check list mentioned above the teacher should see that such children are assessed properly by the experts. Such assessment may be medical and psychological. In most cases experts such as doctors and psychologists are not available for medical and psychological assessment of LD children. In rural areas particularly, trained professionals are not available. In such cases the teacher can conduct functional assessment. Functional assessment which is not a replacement of medical or psychological assessment indicates what a child can do and what he cannot do. Based on functional assessment the teacher can plan and provide specialised service and help in the school. The National Council of Educational Research and Training, New Delhi has developed "Functional Assessment Guide' for use by teachers. After identification and assessment, such children should be placed in an appropriate environment for their education and training. Mildly handicapped children can be placed in regular classroom with provision of resource room help. Severely handicapped children cannot profit from regular classroom instruction. They may be educated and trained by competent professionals in special class settings.

3. Characteristics of LD Children

The LD children constitute a heterogenous group. Some LD children have reading problems and some others have writing problems. Some LD children have problems of comprehension whereas others may have problems in telling the time, locating a place on the map. Thus, it is difficult to mention the characteristics which are noticed in all LD children. The most frequently mentioned characteristics of LD children include the following :

(i) *Ability level* : The ability level of LD children varies from near average to average to above average.

(ii) *Activity level* : The LD children may be either hyperactive or hypoactive. If they are hyperactive they show the following behaviours — constant motor activity, restless, tapping of finger or foot, jumping out of seat, skipping from task to task, etc. If they are hypoactive they fail to react or seem to do everything in slow motion.

(iii) *Attention problems* : The LD children have short attention span; they are easily distractible; they are unable to concentrate on any task for a very long time. They often perseverate. Their attention becomes fixed upon a single task which is repeated over and over; this may be motor or verbal activity.

(iv) *Motor problems* : The LD children are generally clumsy or awkward with poor, fine and gross motor coordination. They demonstrate poor tactile discrimination, excessive need to touch, poor writing and drawing performance.

(v) *Visual perceptual problems* : The LD children are unable to distinguish between visual stimuli (visual discrimination) : they are unable to perceive a figure against a background (visual figure-ground). They are unable to fill in missing parts when only part of a word or object is seen (visual closure); they are also unable to remember and revisualise images or sequences very well (visual memory).

(vi) *Auditory perceptual problems* : The LD children are unable to distinguish between sounds (auditory discrimination) : they are unable to obtain meaning from the spoken word and/or environmental sounds (auditory comprehension). They are unable to attend to important auditory stimuli by pushing all other auditory stimuli into the background (auditory figure-ground). They are unable to fill in missing sounds when only parts of the word are heard (auditory closure); they are also unable to remember auditory stimuli or sequences very well (auditory memory).

(vii) *Language problems* : The LD children demonstrate delayed or slow development of speech articulation, and an inability to organise words to form phrases, clauses, or sentences.

(viii) *Social emotional behaviour problems* : The LD children are impulsive in nature. They fail to think about consequences of their behaviour. At times they exhibit explosive behaviour. They display rage reactions or throw tantrums when crossed. They lack social competence. Their social competence is often below the average for their age and ability. They are unable to adjust to changes. They exhibit rapid mood variation, even from hour to hour.

(ix) *Orientation problems* : The LD children possess poorly developed concept of space, and a distorted body image. They have difficulty in judging distance and size and in discriminating figure from ground, parts from the whole and left from right. They are disoriented in time and experience trouble relating to concepts like before and after, now and then, and today and tomorrow.

(x) *Work habits* : The LD children organise work poorly. They work slowly, and frequently confuse directions or rush through work carelessly.

(xi) *Academic disabilities* : The LD children have problems in reading, arithmetic, writing, spelling, telling time and even locating places on the map.

In general LD children possess these characteristics. But not all LD children demonstrate these characteristics. Some LD children may have one or more such characteristics.

4. Care and Training of LD Children

There are two approaches for the care and treatment of LD children. These are : Medical-Neurological approach and Psycho-Educational approach (Hewett and Forness, 1984).

Medical-Neurological approach : The medical-neurological approach views the LD child as a patient afflicted with minimal brain dysfunction (MBD). Such a child should be treated just like any other individual afflicted with a disease or injury. The most common symptom associated with MBD is hyperactivity. Thus quite logically, medication of some type would be sought to alleviate the child's symptoms. The most widely prescribed drugs to alleviate the symptom of hyperactivity are psychostimulants. Psychostimulants may bring about improvements in the behaviour of the LD child, but their effect on improving the learning of such children is not clearly established by research findings. Psychostimulant drugs can have a positive effect on a child's classroom behaviour, in reducing his activity level and making him more manageable and teachable but we cannot always count on them to remediate the child's learning problems. In addition to psychostimulant drugs, mega-vitamin therapy and diet management are sometimes recommended for LD children. But research findings on the effectiveness of mega-vitamin therapy and diet management are inconclusive. What is needed therefore is a behaviouristic approach or a psycho-educational approach which relies on the teacher's effectiveness in working with such children, motivating them and providing appropriate instruction to them.

Psycho-Educational approach : The psycho-educational approach views the LD child not as a patient but as a learner waiting to be taught. From the psycho-educational perspectives, the LD children are to be identified early, assessed medically and psychologically to arrive at a correct diagnosis of their difficulties and weaknesses and provided with appropriate instruction and training in regular schools, resource rooms, special classes or special schools depending upon their degree of disability. There are various approaches for the education and training of LD. children. All these approaches fall under five categories such as :

Process training

Multisensory approach

Environmental approach

Cognitive training

Other special approaches and activities.

(i) *Process training* : Process training is based on the contention that learning academic subjects requires understanding the underlying psychological processes. Learning disabled children have a disorder in the psychological processes which underlie in understanding or using speech, in reading, writing, arithmetic, etc. Thus it may be of value to train the LD child in the psychological processes which underly various academic subjects. For example, a LD child believed to have reading problems because of difficulties in visual perception will be trained in visual perception.

(ii) *Multisensory approach* : Multisensory approach is based on the assumption that the child will be more likely to learn if more than one of his senses is involved in the learning experiences. One such method is called the VAKT method (V stands for visual, A stands for auditory, K stands for kinesthetic and T stands for tactual). For example, the teacher asks the child to tell a story. The teacher writes down the words of the story on the blackboard. These words serve as material as the child learns to read. In learning the words, the child first sees the word (visual). He hears the teacher say the word (auditory). He says the word (auditory). Finally the child traces the word (kinesthetic and tactual).

(iii) *Environmental approach* : Learning disabled children are usually distractible and hyperactive. For such children an environmental approach is sometimes recommended by some educators. Environmental approach emphasises reducing the irrelevant stimuli in the classroom environment which might distract the child's attention from the learning task. The classroom environment may be modified in the following ways as far as possible and as per necessity to make it free from unnecessary distraction:

— Sound-proofing of walls and ceilings.

- — Carpeting
- — Opaque windows
- — Enclosed book cases and cupboards
- — Limited use of bulletin boards
- — Use of cubicles, three-sided work areas
- — Removing the pictures, calenders and other hanging objects from the walls.
- — Ensuring a noise-free and in other ways a distraction-free environment outside the classroom.
- — Enhancing the intensity of the teaching materials in terms of colour, size, and vividness.

(iv) *Cognitive training* : Many learning disabled children exhibit deficient problem-solving skills. They are likely to act impulsively rather than reflectively, responding quickly without considering the various alternatives. In order to reduce their impulsivity and to increase their reflectivity two techniques are found successful —

(i) Cognitive modelling; and

(ii) Self-instructional training.

Cognitive modelling is sometimes known as meta cognition, meta memory and cognitive behaviour modification strategy. This approach is directed towards providing LD children with an awareness of how people learn or remember. In cognitive modeling the LD child is exposed to models (adults or peers) who tend to be more reflective so that he can imitate the model and learn the appropriate strategy. Through this technique the LD child is taught how to slow himself down before he reads a word or gives an answer, looks carefully at all cues and possibilities, considers his response carefully, and then responds. In remembering, he is taught to group information into small bits or clusters, rehearses these by saying them over and over to himself and even uses mnemonic devices to aid in memory storage. Many LD children improve dramatically when they are simply made aware of the most effective way to learn and remember.

Modeling can also be combined with self-instructional training. In self-instructional training the impulsive child is encouraged to learn to develop verbal control of his behaviour. The following is an example :

- — The teacher (adult model) performs a task (solving an arithmetic problem) while talking out to himself loudly.
- — The child performs the same task under the direction of the teacher.

— The child whispers the instructions to himself as he goes through the task, and finally.

— The child performs the task while guiding his performance via private speech.

Through self-instructional training the LD child is helped to monitor his own performance in learning situation — to be aware of his own approach to cognitive tasks.

(v) *Other special approaches and techniques* : The LD children have characteristics which are unique to them. Although they are not visually impaired they have difficulty in visual perception. They have difficulty in visual reception, visual discrimination, and visual memory. Similarly although they are not auditorily handicapped they have difficulty in auditory awareness, auditory discrimination, and auditory memory. They have problems in attention and retention. These difficulties hinder their acquisition of language, their ability to read and write, listening skills, etc. Hence, special training in these areas is very useful for LD children. The resource teacher can provide such training to the LD children in the resource room. The following approaches and activities are useful :

Listening exercises : The LD children have problems of distractibility which hinder their acquisition of listening skills and hence their ability to follow directions. Listening exercises for such children are often helpful. One exercise involves having someone who is out of sight produce various sounds for the children to identify, such as bouncing a ball, clapping, and shutting a door. Another exercise is, when the group goes for a walk, the children can be instructed to listen for common sounds, including a car running, a train chugging, or a bird singing. To improve comprehension of spoken words in children with listening problems, the teacher can give direction orally, beginning with short and simple ones and increasing the difficulty as the child progresses ('stand up, turn around, and then sit down'). Riddles can also be used to develop listening power and comprehension.

Discrimination learning : The LD children have difficulties in discriminating one letter from another, one word from another and one number from another. Discrimination learning can be encouraged among such children for the above purpose. In discrimination learning children must be trained to attend to the similarities and differences between two letters, words, or numbers (*e.g.*, b, d, p, q; 6, 9; 3, 8; hat, bat etc.) and then to make the correct response. In teaching such children letters, words, or numbers, these are to be written in the beginning in large sizes in crayon on news print paper. The children can trace the letters with their index fingers, while saying the letters, words, or numbers aloud. Visual and auditory attention is thus heightened in relation to these letters, words, or numbers. In order to improve their retention ability repetition or overlearning may be encouraged.

Visual reception training : Visual reception can be encouraged by having children identify common objects by name and tell both their proper use and to whom each object belongs. They can be asked to stand in front of a mirror each day in the resource room and comment on what they see. Children can be given pictures to interpret in terms objects seen, colours, sizes, motion, and other details.

Visual memory training : Visual memory can be developed by having children close their eyes and describe their clothing, a bulletin board in the room, or other children.

Spatial training : Spatial training can be introduced by having children find the top, bottom, sides, and back of an object. The concepts of up, down, over, under, in, bigger, heavier, etc. can be demonstrated.

Auditory awareness training : Auditory awareness can be encouraged by having children remember various types of sounds heard during walk. The children can identify the source of each sound and give it an appropriate label. The teacher can hold a wrist watch to a child's ear at varying distances and train the child to listen and to raise a hand when the ticking is no longer audible. Directions can be whispered to the child at varying distances from each ear. Quiet periods can be held during which children are asked to listen to various sounds.

Auditory discrimination exercises : Auditory discrimination exercises can include hiding a ticking clock and asking a child to point to the direction of the clock. The teacher can tap several times on the desk and have the children listen, count to themselves and report the number of taps. While blind folded, a child can identify a classmate by his voice.

Auditory memory and sequencing training : Auditory memory and sequencing can be developed by asking children to repeat directions, phone numbers, and clapping patterns. They can listen to nursery rhymes and songs and pick out details they will be asked to repeat afterwards. The teacher can tell simple jokes and have the children repeat them.

Remedial instruction : The children with learning disability are benefited mostly from remedial instruction. Remedial instruction is nothing but good teaching with two definite and specific objectives, such as :

(i) Eliminating ineffective habits and reteaching skills which have been incorrectly learned. This refers to remediation of defects.

(ii) Teaching for the first time those habits, skills and behaviours which have never been learned but should have been learned by the child to acquire academic skills. This refers to developmental teaching or development of increased competencies.

Remedial instruction requires proper diagnosis of a child's abilities and disabilities in specific school subjects, identifying skills and processes which require remediation, and then providing him just good teaching in areas of his weaknesses through systematic planning, individualised instruction, tutoring in one-to-one or small group situation, evaluating his progress periodically and if necessary reteaching, encouraging intensive drill, practice or repetition and modifying the programme and adopting alternate materials and methods, using work-books, supplementary materials and multisensory approach. Most LD children improve their performance dramatically after exposure to remedial instruction in resource rooms which seemed difficult in regular classroom settings. Remedial instruction in the resource room can vary from one hour every day to a half-day's programme regularly depending upon deficiencies and the amount of training required. It is to be emphasized that the sooner the remedial instruction starts in the elementary school the easier for the child to compensate his deficiencies and the better for his later progress in upper classes.

5. Role of The Teacher

Managing the LD children : The child with learning disabilities needs individual tutoring in one or more of his areas of disability. Whether or not there is a resource teacher available will determine to a great extent how much of this instruction will be assumed by the regular class teacher. It is a fact that the regular classroom teacher and the resource teacher should have a cooperative working relationship. The regular teacher should work out with the resource teacher exactly what the duties of each of them are. "Who will be responsible for what" is a basic question that is sometimes never decided. However, the regular teacher has the following role to play :

(1) The regular classroom teacher who deals with children — abled and disabled — has much opportunity to observe their behavioural characteristics, identify the LD children and refer the suspected cases to the resource teacher for taking steps for assessment and diagnosis of their difficulties and deficiencies.

(2) Once he is sure of the specific deficiencies of such children he should plan his instruction in a systematic and sensitive way in consultation with the resource teacher. If there is no resource teacher in his school he must plan everything himself. He should remember that what LD children need is just good teaching. What is good teaching for LD children is also good teaching for normal children. There are many ways to describe good teaching for normal as well as LD children. The following principles may serve as guidelines for the regular teacher teaching normal and LD children in integrated settings (Hewett and forness, 1984).

(i) Expect the child to learn : Teacher's expectation is reflected in the child's performance.

(ii) Take nothing for granted : Understand the child very patiently and carefully. The LD child may pretend to be attentive, motivated and seem to understand everything you are talking about, but in reality he does not.

(iii) Bombard the senses : Use multisensory approach to involve the child more completely in the teaching learning process.

(iv) Load up the cues : Have the child label and describe what is happening. Use a variety of distinctive elements and change them from time to time to bring novelty in experiences.

(v) Make it vivid : Increase the intensity of what is given to the child. Make it bigger, louder, more colourful, more imaginative, more exciting and more interesting. Be enthusiastic and animated.

(vi) Repeat as often as necessary : Assess the child's level of understanding. Be sure you have reached the child's level. Ask the child to tell you what have been presented. Repeat statements. Repeat directions. Don't be boring.

(vii) Make it relevant : Enter the child's world, Leave the examples given in the prescribed text books. Give them content that is familiar to them and part of their out-of-school life. Introduce local specific elements in your presentation.

(viii) Make it concrete : Use pictures, recordings and spoken words. These are fine. But don't stop there. Show real objects. Let the child touch, smell, manipulate and get a direct impression and experience about concepts you are presenting.

(ix) Surprise the child : Present novel experiences. Use different materials and methods. Excite the child with stimulating experiences.

(x) Emphasize the positive achievement : Ignore the mistakes and at best make the child understand his mistakes, but in all cases recognise his positive achievements and tell it to others.

(xi) Move sequentially : Teach step by step.

(xii) Review objectively : Look back. Introspect what was your expectation. Modify your strategy and get ready to move ahead again as soon as possible.

(xiii) Make it distraction-free : Remove irrelevant stimuli from the classroom. Have distraction-free physical environment in and out of the classroom.

(xiv) Be a mother : Show motherly love. Take their care. Win their heart and you will win the battle.

(xv) Be open to your colleagues : Cooperate with them and seek their cooperation. Share and exchange experiences and learn from other's experiences.

Williams and Hounshell (1998) in their article *Enabling the Learning Disabled.* Teaching Strategies for challenged students say, "Many LD (learning disabled) students have the academic potential of non-disabled students but require some assistance in unveiling their potential and turning it into achievement".

Teaching Strategies

— One of the most important things teachers should do is to provide support for risk taking and call attention to the successful work of an LD student without attaching the LD label.

— Making use of technology is advantageous, and it is a good idea to use computers as often as possible. Computers stimulate a variety of senses for LD students and are valuable.

— LD students are particularly receptive to television and video because they appeal to a number of senses.

— The music sounds and graphic often make learning come to life for LD students.

— LD students feel safe when they are watching a movie because there is no fear of being called on to answer a question or read aloud.

Classroom Organization : Teachers of LD students should also structure class time so that intense, laborious activities are interspersed with relaxing, enjoyable activities that allow students to move around. The teacher should take care of the following points.

Seating Arrangement

— Desks arranged in clusters, however, are more conducive to promoting children's discussion or collaboration.

— When introducing new vocabulary words, repetition is important.

— To avoid confusing the child, teachers should plan assignments that focus on a primary task.

— It is better to start simply and add layers of complexity to LD students' assignments as the school year progresses.

Assessment Strategies

— When assessing LD students, teachers should make assignments clear and grade using a qualitative scoring rubric. At the same time, when administering multiple choice tests, it is important that the answer choices are clear and that one choice stands out as the best answer.

Building Confidence : An excellent way to help LD students who are struggling with problems of low self-esteem is to entrust them with some duties and responsibilities. Taking care of a pet or a plant makes students feel important. They will see that their presence in the class is important not only in terms of potential academic contribution but also in maintaining the life of an organism. This attitude of the teacher will bring a dramatic shift in students' self-confidence.

8

Integrating the Emotionally Disturbed

1. Who are the Emotionally Disturbed Children?

There is no universally accepted definition of emotionally disturbed children. Professional groups and experts dealing with disturbed children have constructed individual working definitions to fit their own professional purposes. Defining the disturbed child is like defining experiences such as, anger, loneliness, or happiness. One can understand what these experiences are but defining these experiences is far from simple.

One current definition that is particularly relevant for special education is that offered by Bower (1969). Bower states that 'emotionally disturbed' children are those who exhibit one more of the following characteristics to a marked extent and over a period of time :

(i) An inability to learn which cannot be explained in terms of intellectual, sensory or health factors;

(ii) An inability to build or maintain satisfactory interpersonal relationship with peers and teachers;

(iii) Inappropriate types of behaviour or feelings under normal conditions;

(iv) A general pervasive mood or unhappiness or depression and

(v) A tendency to develop physical symptoms, pains, or fears associated with personal or school problems.

The emotionally disturbed child behaves in ways which are socially unacceptable and personally unsatisfying. Many normal children manifest disturbed behaviours during the course of growing up. But what separates emotionally disturbed children from normal children is :

(i) The frequency of their disturbed behaviour.

(ii) Its degree of severity.

(iii) Its duration.

(iv) The number of disturbed behaviours found collectively in a single child.

The four criteria just mentioned above also suggest that emotional disturbance may be of severe type or it may be of mild and moderate type. At present there is no consensus as to what behaviours qualify as mildly or moderately disturbed. In fact it depends upon how much teachers and others tolerate about deviant behaviour of the disturbed child. Thus, it is rightly said "exactly what constitutes mildly or moderately disturbed behaviours exists largely in the eyes of the beholder". It is no doubt a fact that disturbed behaviours which are transients in nature and observed in some children in the early grades but not later on come under mild or moderate category.

Types of Emotionally Disturbed Children. Emotionally disturbed children are sometimes known as problem children. Depending upon the type of problems exhibited such children are classified into three categories such as :

Children with Conduct Problem

Children with Personality Problem

Children with Inadequacy — Immaturity Problem.

The behaviour traits and life history characteristics of such children are given below (Hallahan and Kauffman, 1978).

Conduct Problem

Behaviour traits — Disobedience
Disruptiveness
Fighting
Destructiveness
Temper tantrums
Irresponsibility
Impertinent
Jealous
Anger
Bossy
Profanity
Attention seeking
Boisterous

Life History Characteristics — Assaultive
Defies authority
Inadequate guilt feelings
Quarrelsome

Personality Problem

Behaviour traits — Feelings of inferiority
Self-consciousness
Social withdrawal
Anxiety
Crying
Hypersensitive
Seldom smiles
Chews finger nails
Depression
Chronic sadness
Shyness

Life history Characteristics — Seclusive
Shy
Sensitive
Worries
Timid
Has anxiety over own behaviour.

Inadequacy — Immaturity Problem

Behaviour traits — Preoccupation
Short attention span
Clumsiness
Passivity
Day dreaming
Sluggish
Drowsiness
Prefers younger play mates
Masturbation

Giggles
Easily flustered
Chews objects
Picked on by others
Plays with toys in class.

Life history Characteristics — Habitually truant from home
Unable to cope with a complex world
Incompetent, immature
Engages in furtive stealing.

2. Identification and Placement

(i) *Identification is easier* : While there is a problem defining and classifying various types of emotional disturbance, it is much easier to identify disturbed behaviours. Most disturbed children do not typically escape notice. The most common type of disturbed children — children with conduct problem — readily attract attention with their behaviour. So there is seldom any real problem in identifying them. Immature children and those with personality problems may be less abrasive, but they are not extremely difficult to recognize. Disturbed children are so readily identified by school personnel that few authorities bother to carry out systematic screening procedure. Moreover, special education services for disturbed children lag far behind the need. There is not much point in screening children for problems when the services available to treat these problems is inadequate.

(ii) *Early identification* : One important point to remember is that the younger the child, the more difficult it is to judge whether or not his behaviour is disturbed. Some disturbed children go unnoticed because teachers are not sensitive to their problems or their environment. Some sensitive teachers make errors in their judgements about the disturbed behaviour of children. Some disturbed children also do not exhibit disturbed behaviours in the school. In spite of these problems, disturbed children are to be identified early so that suitable intervention programmes can be planned for them.

(iii) *Identification procedure* : What techniques are to be adopted for screening and identifying disturbed children? There are two important considerations to be kept in mind while discussing about the screening and identification of disturbed children. First, there is not an adequate definition of the disturbed child. Second, there are no adequate instruments or measuring emotional disturbance. Hence, identification of disturbed children depends on subjective judgement as mentioned below :

(i) Informal teacher judgement.

(ii) Teacher's ratings of children's behaviour.

(iii) Children's ratings of their peers and their own behaviour.

(iv) Direct observation by teachers.

Teachers and peers are in a better position to observe the behaviour of the disturbed child than the psychologist or the psychiatrist. When teachers are required to directly observe the troublesome behaviour of a child the following considerations are to be kept in mind :

(i) It must be pin-pointed.

(ii) It must be recorded accurately.

(iii) The number and frequency of occurrence of the behaviours should be noted.

(iv) The behaviour should be recorded over an extended period of time.

(v) The child should be considered carefully as a whole person.

(vi) The child's behaviour should be observed directly and recorded quantitatively by more than one teacher.

Depending on the type of problem behaviour the child exhibits, a variety of diagnostic procedures may be used. Hyperactive children may be referred to a pediatrician who may prescribe drug treatment for them. Children who appear seriously disturbed may be referred to a psychologist or psychiatrist for consultation. A psychologist may also administer projective personality tests to get children reveal their inner conflicts.

All these approaches should be directed towards gaining a clearer understanding of the children's difficulties and eventually providing a more adequate and successful school experiences for them in the regular schools.

3. Characteristics of Emotionally Disturbed Children

Emotionally disturbed children may be either of mild and moderate type or of severe type. Teachers in regular schools are expected to manage the mildly and moderately disturbed children in their classrooms. Hence, it is imperative for them to be familiar with the behavioural and psychological characteristics of mildly and moderately disturbed children. We will discuss the behavioural and psychological characteristics of mildly and moderately disturbed children under two heads :

Intelligence and Achievement, and

Social and Emotional Characteristics.

Intelligence and Achievement

(i) In general, mildly and moderately disturbed children are found to be dull. Their IQ falls around 90. Very few disturbed children are found to be bright.

(ii) Most severely disturbed children are untestable. Those who can be tested are found to be retarded, their IQ falling around 50.

(iii) There are some disturbed children who are extremely bright, but they are not representative of disturbed children as a group.

(iv) The lower IQ scores of disturbed children are consistent with their impairment in other areas of functioning.

(v) Most disturbed children are underachievers at school. A disturbed child does not achieve at the level expected for his mental age. It is relatively seldom that one finds an academically advanced disturbed child. Most severely disturbed children lack even the most basic reading and arithmetic skills. Those who appear to be competent in reading or arithmetic are usually unable to apply their skills in any useful way to everyday problems.

Social and Emotional Characteristics

(i) Conduct disorders are the most common problems exhibited by disturbed children. Hitting, fighting, yelling, refusal to comply with requests, crying, destructiveness, vandalism are most commonly exhibited by such children.

(ii) They drive adults to distraction with their bad temperament and nastiness.

(iii) They are not popular among their normal peers. They are not good at making friends. Their most obvious problem is a failure to establish close and satisfying emotional ties with other people.

(iv) Some disturbed children are withdrawn. Their drawing back from interaction with others — their social isolation is clearly self-imposed. When well meaning adults and others care about them and try to help them, such children strike out with hostility and aggression. It is easy to see why they are friendless. They are abusive, destructive, unpredictable, irresponsible, bossy, quarrelsome, irritable, jealous, defiant — anything but pleasant and nice to be with. Naturally other children and adults choose not to spend their time with this kind of person.

(v) Their behaviour is not only extremely troublesome but also resistant to change through the usual means of discipline. Often they are so frequently reprimanded and punished that punishment means little or nothing for them.

4. Educational Programme

How should disturbed children be educated? There are many different answers to the question of educating disturbed children. This is natural because disturbed behaviours range from aggression to withdrawal and from mild to profound category. There are different approaches to the education of disturbed children such as :

Psychoanalytic approach,

Psychoeducational approach,

Humanistic approach,

Ecological approach and

Behavioural approach.

We will not go deep into the differences in these approaches but, instead, highlight on the essential points of these approaches.

(i) Emotional disturbance is the result of some inner conflict. Hence, before any educational programme is designed for these children psychologists and psychiatrists must help to uncover the underlying inner conflict in an effort to improve the psychological functioning as well as behaviour and achievement of the child.

(ii) Emphasis should be placed on teacher-pupil relationship in which the child feels accepted and free to act out his impulses in a permissive environment. Initially little emphasis should be given on academic achievement or to change the 'surface behaviour' of the child. If the teacher can uncover the mental conflict half of his work is achieved.

(iii) Once the underlying pathology is revealed the teacher should gradually move towards managing the disturbed behaviour and academic achievement. There should be emphasis on meeting the individual needs of children and most teaching should be done through projects or the creative arts like music, art, dance, etc.

(iv) Educational programmes should be designed to enhance children's self-direction, self-evaluation and active involvement in the learning environment. The teachers should be non-authoritarian, open and personal in their approach towards the child.

(v) The roots of emotional disturbance may lie in the social environment of the child in which the child lives, grows and interacts. Hence, the entire social system — the school, family, community and other social agencies must be altered as far as practicable. Hence, the teacher's concern should not be just effective teaching in the classroom but to work with the child's family, neighbourhood and community agencies as well. Teacher's rapport with parents, community members and other adults will help to achieve his goal-altering the social system.

(vi) Educational practices must emphasize the behaviour modification strategies. School authorities must remember that every behaviour is learned. The disturbed child has failed to learn desirable behaviour and has learned inappropriate behaviours. Following the behaviour modification techniques the teacher can modify the undesirable behaviours of the child, teach him desirable behaviour through praise, reward, and recognition and develop in him the ability and confidence in learning essential academic and other skills.

(vii) The mildly and moderately disturbed children should be kept in the mainstream as much as possible. If it is not feasible to keep the disturbed child in regular classes all the time then he may be removed to the resource room or the special class for a part of the day with the goal of reintegration in the regular classes.

(viii) The curriculum for such children will be the same as for normal children with emphasis on basic academic skills (reading, writing and arithmetic), art, music, dance, social skills, and affective experiences. How to manage his own feelings and behaviour and how to get along with other people are essential skills which are no less important as academic skills. Teachers are expected to adopt novel teaching methods based on their experiences for teaching these skills.

(ix) The basic idea in the education of disturbed children is that they can be re-educated if the social system is changed and if teachers play their role with sincerity and dedication.

5. Role of the Teacher

There are specially trained resource teachers for all categories of disabled children, but trained resource teachers are not available for teaching emotionally disturbed children. It is, therefore, obvious that disturbed children are to be educated in regular classrooms by regular teachers. Regular teachers are, therefore, to play a very befitting role in managing such children :

(i) If there is an emotionally disturbed child in the regular class the regular teacher must ask the special educator or any other special education personnel for advice concerning behaviour management, behaviour modification and teaching technique.

(ii) The regular teacher should let the child know from the first contact that he expects a reasonable standard of conduct to be maintained. The sooner the child knows the limits of permissible conduct, the better.

(iii) It is essential that the teacher communicates his expectations to the child clearly and firmly. Nothing is to be gained by beating around the bush or keeping the child guessing about what the teacher has in mind regarding behaviour and goals.

(iv) The teacher must have realistic expectations concerning the child's behaviour and academic performance. His tasks should be well within his capacity, but still a challenging. The child must feel success and pride in what he accomplishes.

(v) It is important that the teacher empathizes with the child and understands how negative aspects of his social environment (abuse at home, peers who taunt him, teachers who criticise him) may contribute to his inappropriate behaviour. If negative environmental influences can be identified he should try to change them, if possible.

(vi) The teacher must be able to tolerate a great deal of unpleasantness and rejection. He should not be counter-aggressive or with drawing himself. Some disturbed children change dramatically by the kind gesture of the teacher. But this may not be the case always. Kind gestures, caring attitude and decent behaviour of the teacher are not always reciprocated by his pupils. Still then the teacher needs to maintain considerable patience which most teachers are not capable of.

(vii) There must be consistent and appropriate consequences for behaviour. The child's desirable behaviour should be immediately recognised and rewarded with praise and signs of approval. Inappropriate behaviour is to be consistently ignored or, if necessary, may be handled with mild punishment. Recognition and praise for good behaviour should be given openly so that other students can see and hear the teacher. If it is necessary to reprimand the child this should be done as quietly and privately as possible.

(viii) The teacher managing emotionally disturbed children should remember that good behaviour management for disturbed children has a lot in common with good behaviour management for all children. The best preventive action any teacher can take is to make sure that the classroom is a happy place where children take pride in their work and learn to treat others with respect.

(ix) Most behaviour problems in the classroom are noticed when children don't find interest in their education; when they fail to get any real meaning of their schooling; when the quality of teaching is poor. Good teachers do not encounter much problem behaviour in their classrooms. Good teachers are not simply teachers; they are teacher-counsellors. They impress upon the students through their qualitative teaching, effective counselling, and pleasing personality.

"A teacher-counsellor is a decent adult, educated, well trained; able to give and receive affection; to live relaxed, and to be firm; a professional through and through; a person with a sense of the significance of time, of the usefulness of today and the promise of tomorrow; a person of hope, quiet confidence, and joy; one who has committed himself to children and to the proposition that children who are emotionally disturbed can be helped by the process of re-education".

9

Education of Gifted Children

1. Who are the Gifted Children?

There is no unanimous agreement about the definition of giftedness. The profusion of definitions of giftedness is great which is probably due to the fact there are many kinds of gifted children. Moreover, each culture defines giftedness in its own image, in terms of the abilities that the culture values. For example, ancient Greeks honoured the philosopher and the orator; and Romans valued the engineer and the soldier.

Giftedness has been traditionally associated with intellectual superiority — a very high IQ score on a standardized test of intelligence. Over the past few decades, periodic efforts have been made to broaden the definition of giftedness to include more than abilities directly related to school work. As for instance, Marland (1972) defined gifted students as follows : "Gifted and talented children are those identified by professionally qualified persons who, by virtue of outstanding abilities, are capable of high performance. These are children who require differentiated programmes and services beyond those normally provided by the regular school programmes in order to realize their contributions to self and society. Children capable of high performance include those with demonstrated achievement and/or potential ability in any one of the following areas :

(i) General intellectual ability.

(ii) Specific academic aptitude.

(iii) Creative or productive thinking.

(iv) Leadership ability.

(v) Visual and performing arts.

One of the latest definitions of giftedness has been given by Ross (1993). According to Ross, "Children and youth with outstanding talent perform, or show the potential for performing, at reasonably high levels of accomplishments when compared with others of their age, experience, or environment. These children and youth exhibit high performance capability in intellectual, creative, and/or artistic areas, possess an unusual leadership capacity or excel in specific academic fields. They require services or activities not ordinarily provided by the schools. Outstanding talents are present in children and youth from all cultural groups, across all economic strata, and in all areas of human endeavour."

Other definitions of giftedness try to include the way an individual, defines and then tackles a problem — the ability to *problem-find* and *problem-solve* (Gardner, 1985; Seigler, 1985; Sternberg, 1986). In the real world, problems do not come in neat packages ready for solving. Usually they are hard to define and organise. Problems in the real world are ill-structured. The ability to take an ill-structured problem and organise it so that the issue is clear is one indicator of giftedness. Thus, "gifted students are those who demonstrate or show the potential for outstanding performance in academic, creative, artistic, leadership or problem-solving areas and who require special education and related services to actualize their potentialities and maximize their capacities."

2. Identification of Gifted Children

Our society has a special interest in children who are gifted. As individuals, they have the same right to appropriate education as do all children. In addition, many of the leaders, scientists, engineers and doctors of the 21st century will come from the current group of gifted children. This necessiates early identification of gifted children and provision of suitable education and other services for them.

Gifted children are usually identified by subjective and objective method, such as the following :

Intelligence Scores

Creativity Measures

Achievement Measures

Measures of Special Aptitude (such as in Mathematics)

Nomination of Peers

Nomination by Parents

Self-Nomination.

It is important to note that no single method can identify all gifted and talented children. A combination of subjective and objective methods is desirable for identifying gifted and talented children.

Identification Checklist for Parents. Parents can identify their gifted children before they enter the primary school with the help of the following checklist as suggested by Witty (1955). Such identification/ nomination by parents should be followed by systematic assessment by specialists.

(i) The early use of a large and accurately employed vocabulary.

(ii) The use of entire sentences and ability to tell or reproduce a story at an early date.

(iii) Keen observation and retention of information about things observed.

(iv) Interest in and liking for books.

(v) Early interest in calenders, telling time, and clocks.

(vi) The ability to attend or concentrate for a longer period than is usual for children.

(vii) Demonstration of proficiency in drawing, music, or other art form.

(viii) Interest in exploration and discovery of cause and effect relationships.

(ix) The early development of ability to read.

Identification Checklist for Teachers. The classroom teacher has the primary responsibility of identifying the gifted children. He is in a better position than anyone else to observe the classroom behaviour of children. In order to make the teacher's observation/nomination more systematic Koogh and De Haan (1955) have suggested the following checklist :

(i) Learns rapidly and easily.

(ii) Uses a lot of common sense and practical knowledge.

(iii) Reasons things out, thinks clearly, recognizes relationships and comprehends meanings.

(iv) Retains what he has heard or read without much drill.

(v) Knows about many things of which other children are unaware.

(vi) Can read books that are one to two years in advance of the rest of the class.

(vii) Performs difficult mental tasks.

(viii) Asks many questions.

(ix) Does some academic work one to two years in advance of the rest of the class.

(x) Is original, uses good but unusual methods or ideas.

(xi) Is alert, keenly observant and responds quickly.

It is important to note that nomination by a group of teachers is more valid than nomination by a single teacher. In any case identification/

nomination by teachers should be followed by objective methods of identification and assessment by specialists.

3. Characteristics of Gifted Children

Giftedness is a complex concept covering a wide range of abilities and traits. Some children have special talents. They may not be outstanding in academics, but they may have special abilities in areas such as music, art, dance, or leadership. Other children may have intellectual abilities found only in 1 child in 1,000 or 1 child in 10,000.

Clark (1988) describes the characteristics of gifted children across five domains : cognitive, affective, physical, intuitive, and societal. There are individual differences among gifted children relating to these characteristics. These characteristics are given below :

I. The Cognitive Domain

- Extraordinary quantity of information; unusual retentiveness.
- Advanced comprehension.
- Unusually varied interests and curiosity.
- High level of language development.
- High level of verbal ability.
- High level of visual and spatial ability.
- Unusual capacity for processing information.
- Accelerated pace of thought processes.
- Flexible thought process.
- Comprehensive synthesis.
- Early ability to delay closure.
- Heightened capacity for seeing unusual and diverse relationships and overall gestalt.
- Ability to generate original ideas and solutions.
- Early differential patterns for thought processing (*e.g.*, thinking in alternatives and abstract terms, sensing consequences, making generalizations).
- Early ability to use and form conceptual frameworks.
- An evaluative approach toward oneself and others.

- Persistent goal-directed behaviour.

II. The Affective Domain

- Large accumulation of information about emotions that have not been brought to awareness.
- Unusual sensitivity to the expectations and feelings of others.
- Keen sense of humour — may be gentle or hostile.
- Heightened self-awareness, accompanied by feelings of being "different".
- Idealism and a sense of justice that appear at an early age.
- Earlier development of an inner locus of control and satisfaction.
- Advanced levels on moral judgment.
- High expectations of self and others, which often lead to high levels of frustration with self, others, and situations.
- Unusual emotional depth and intensity.
- Sensitivity to inconsistency between ideals and behaviour.

III. The Physical Domain

- Unusual discrepancy between physical and intellectual development.
- Low tolerance for the lag between their standards and their physical capacity.
- Cartesian split — can include neglect of physical well-being and avoidance of physical activity.

IV. The Intuitive Domain

- Early involvement and concern for intuitive knowing, psychic and metaphysical phenomena.
- Open to experiences in this area; will experiment with psi and metaphysical phenomena.
- Creativity apparent in all areas of endeavour.
- Acceptance and expression of a high

		level of intuitive ability, especially with the highly gifted.
V. The Societal Domain	♦	Strongly motivated by self-actualization needs.
	♦	Advanced cognitive and affective capacity for conceptualizing and solving societal problems.

Source : From *Growing Up Gifted Developing the Potential of Children at Home and at School* (3rd ed.) (pp. 253, 260, 264, 268, 271) by B. Clark, 1988 Columbus. OH: Merrill.

Non-Intellectual Factors of Giftedness. Over the past few decades it has been realised that superior intelligence alone does not lead to outstanding performance. Giftedness is the product of the interaction between cognitive and non-cognitive factors. Gifted students possess both cognitive characteristics and non-cognitive characteristics such as affective, intuitive, physical and societal (Clark, 1988).

Retrospective Study by Bloom : Benjamin Bloom and his colleagues (1985) attempted to uncover the factors that are linked to extraordinary ability. Bloom conducted a retrospective study of the early life of world class swimmers, pianists, mathematicians and other persons who are gifted. In interview with the subjects, their parents and their former teachers, he found that "several general characteristics seem important whatever the talent area :

(1) Willingness to do great amount of work to achieve a high level of standard.

(2) Competitiveness with peers in the area of talent and determination to do the best at all costs.

(3) Ability to rapidly learn new techniques, ideas, or processes in their area of talent."

Bloom (1985) suggested that the group's high motivation was stimulated in a powerful way by the early recognition of talent by parents and friends, who went out of their way to obtain special instruction and to encourage and nurture the talent. The enthusiasm and support of the family seemed to be a critical element in the emergence of these gifted persons into world class performers.

Retrospective Study of Cox, Daniel and Boston : Studies by Cox, Daniel and Boston (1985) indicate the role of the family in producing gifted children. "They are singled out at an early age for their accomplishments in arts and sciences. When asked about the major influences on their lives, they paid tribute to their parents. Virtually all the parents had let their children know the value of learning through personal example."

"The parents supported without pushing. Their homes had books, journals and newspapers. They took the children to the library. The parents themselves read, and they read to their children. Most important, they respected their children's ideas."

Another strong influence on these students was their teachers. If children do not receive the support of their families, the school and individual teachers have a responsibility to recognise and help them develop their special ability.

Longitudinal Study of Terman : Terman (1959) conducted longitudinal studies of gifted students and found the following non-intellective factors of giftedness :

(1) They are less prone to overstatement or cheating.

(2) They appear superior on tests of emotional stability.

(3) They have broad range of interests in abstract subjects (literature, history and mathematics).

(4) They are above average in physique and health.

Longitudinal Study of White and Renzulli : White and Renzulli (1987) conducted a longitudinal study on gifted children. They found school experiences to be instrumental in nurturing giftedness. They found the following factors of giftedness :

(1) Peer interaction

(2) Exposure to competitions

(3) Creating a strong desire to excel.

Studies by Terman and Oden : Terman and Oden (1947) compared a group of 150 gifted men who had not achieved to the level of their apparent ability. In their self-ratings and in the ratings by their wives and parents, four main factors separated the underachieving men from the achieving men :

(1) Greater feelings of inferiority.

(2) Less self-confidence.

(3) Less perseverance.

(4) Less of a sense of life goals.

Their study indicate that self-confidence, perseverance, a desire to excel and clear life goals coupled with intellectual superiority contribute to giftedness.

Studies by Whitmore : Whitmore (1980) summed up the literature on the distinctive personality and behavioural traits of gifted underachievers and found that "intellectual superiority is not enough for outstanding performance in any line of human endeavour. In addition to intellectual superiority, a strong positive self-concept, high self-esteem, expectation of success, control over one's own actions and emotional stability contribute to giftedness."

Renzulli's views : Renzulli (1977) who is an authority on the psychology of giftedness says; "Gifted are those who have demonstrated —

(1) High ability (including high intelligence).

(2) High creativity (the ability to formulate novel ideas and apply them to the solution of problems).

(3) High task commitment (a high level of motivation and the ability to see a project through to its completion).

Renzulli (1977) is of the view that all three factors — high ability, high creativity, and high motivation are necessary for truly gifted performance in any field.

To sum up, the following non-intellective factors seem important for giftedness :

(i) Emotional stability.

(ii) Broad range of interests.

(iii) Self-confidence.

(iv) Positive self-concept.

(v) High self-esteem.

(vi) High task commitment.

(vii) A desire to excel.

(viii) Willingness to do great amount of work.

(ix) Perserverance.

(x) Competitiveness.

(xi) Experience of success.

(xii) Peer interaction.

(xiii) A sense of life goals.

(xiv) Control over one's own action.

(xv) Objectivity.

(xvi) Leadership ability.

(xvii) High ethical and moral behaviour.

(xviii) Superior physique and health.

(xix) High creativity.

In addition to these non-cognitive factors certain factors in the home and school environment are also very important for nurturing giftedness :

(i) Early recognition of talent in the home and school.

(ii) Early provision of special instruction in the home.

(iii) Provision of enrichment materials in the school.

(iv) Guidance by parents and teachers.

(v) Encouragement by teachers and parents.

(vi) Moral and financial support by parents.

(vii) Exemplary behaviour of parents.

Giftedness is the result of interplay between intellectual factors and non-intellectual factors under conducive conditions in the home and school.

4. Educational Programmes for the Gifted

Aims of Education of the Gifted. In a broader sense, the aims of education of the gifted are no different from those for all other children. Feelings of self-worth, self-sufficiency, civic responsibilities, and vocational competence are important for everyone. There are, however, some additional goals which are especially desirable for gifted and talented children. Gallagher (1981) has suggested two major objectives of educational programmes for the gifted and talented children :

(i) Mastering the knowledge structure of disciplines which includes basic principles and systems of knowledge.

(ii) Heuristic skills which include problem-solving, creativity, and use of the scientific methods.

Setting educational goals for gifted children means little unless these children are given appropriate learning opportunities, or unless the school programmes are modified to match their special needs. The school programme for the gifted can be modified in three areas : learning environments, content, and cognitive strategies (Kirk, Gallagher and Anastasiow (1996).

Modification in the Learning Environment. The learning environment can be modified for the gifted and talented students in three ways. These are :

(i) Flexible Pacing,

(ii) Grouping and

(iii) Special Courses.

(i) *Flexible Pacing* : Flexible pacing is a strategy that accelerates the student to a level in the school programme that is higher than the level of his/her age-mates. This strategy involves the following :

— Early admission in the school or college.

— Continuous progress at one's own rate.

— Skipping (bypassing) subjects and receiving some instruction at a higher level with another group of students while remaining with the peer group for most of the instruction.

— Skipping grades (double promotion).

— Concurrent (dual) enrolment at two levels — secondary and post-secondary.

— Giving credit on satisfactory completion of an examination.

— Covering the course in a shortened period of time and pursuing special courses during the rest of the time.

(ii) *Grouping* : Students can be grouped on the basis of performance or aptitude. Having all students with high performance ability in one group allows the teacher to proceed much more swiftly and in greater depth. Grouping can be of various types :

— Cross-age or multi-age grouping of students on the basis of similar interests or skills.

— Homogenous grouping of students in a particular class on the basis of similar skill level.

— Cluster grouping within a regular class in which a cluster group (4 to 10) of students receives academic support from the cluster teacher.

— Subject grouping in which students are grouped for specific subjects on the basis of their performance or aptitude in that subject.

— Part-time placement in the regular class with part-time placement in a special class for specialized instruction.

— Full-time placement in a special class.

(iii) *Special Courses* : At the secondary level, special courses can be organised for gifted and talented students. These include :

— Honours courses.

— Advanced placement courses or college level courses.

— International courses and foreign languages.

— Special school courses.

— Residential high school courses not available in most high schools.

Modification of Content. Boredom is a real problem for gifted students because they are forced to learn material they already know. For this reason, the teacher needs to —

— find out what the students know before instruction,

— arrange to teach, in a brief fashion, the remaining concepts or skills, and

— provide a different set of experiences to enrich or advance the students.

Content modification involves the following :

(i) Content Acceleration,

(ii) Content Enrichment,

(iii) Content Sophistication, and

(iv) Content Novelty.

(i) *Content acceleration* : This process allows students to master increasingly complex set of ideas at a faster rate. For example, by learning calculus in ninth grade, students have the foundation to begin physics and chemistry which require the skills of calculus.

(ii) *Content enrichment* : This process gives students the opportunity for a greater appreciation of the topic under study by expanding the material — exploring additional examples, using specific illustrations, taking additional assignments, referring to encyclopaedia, etc.

(iii) *Content sophistication* : This process involves challenging students who are gifted to use higher levels of thinking to understand ideas that average students of the same age would find difficult or impossible to comprehend. The objective is to encourage gifted children to understand important abstractions, scientific laws, and general principles that can be applied in many circumstances.

(iv) *Consent novelty* : Content novelty is the introduction of material that normally would not appear in the general curriculum because of time constraints or the abstract nature of the content. Computers can be used to introduce content novelty into the curriculum.

Teaching Cognitive Strategies. One objective of all educators of gifted and talented students is to increase or enhance their capability in problem finding and problem solving. Problem finding is the ability to review an area of study and to perceive those elements worthy of further analysis and study. Problem solving is the ability to reach a previously determined answer by organising and processing the available information in a logical and systematic fashion. Along with enhancing their problem finding and problem solving skills, gifted and talented students should be guided to extend their intellectual fluency through *brain storming*. The four ground rules for brain storming are as follows :

(i) No criticism should be allowed when a student presents an idea.

(ii) The more ideas the better.

(iii) Students should be encouraged to integrate and combine ideas.

(iv) Evaluation should take place after all ideas have been presented.

5. Role of the Teacher

No educational programme is more important than the teacher who implements it. Most schools do not get the services of a specialist teacher for educating gifted and talented students. Hence, the regular teacher has to play an important role in identifying children who are gifted, assessing their potentialities, modifying the learning environment, providing acceleration and enrichment and organise brain storming sessions for gifted students.

One of the first questions most people ask is whether the teacher must be gifted to teach gifted children effectively. The answer is 'Not Necessarily'. In fact all teachers must be gifted, regardless of whom they teach. They should be gifted in different ways to teach different children. Nonetheless, teachers of gifted children do need some particular qualities. They must :

— be willing to accept unusual and diverse questions, answers and projects;

— be intellectually curious;

— be systematic and business like;

— be well prepared in instructional techniques;

— be well prepared in content areas;

— have a variety of interests;

— appreciate achievements;

— realize that they may not know as much about some topics as the children, and be comfortable with that situation.

(Heward and Orlansky, 1992)

6. Underachieving Gifted Children

Some children with superior intellectual ability don't perform well in school. Some gifted students actually fail in school. In such cases there is a discrepancy between their potentialities and their actual performance. They are called the underachieving gifted children.

Terman and Oden (1947) found four major factors of underachievement of gifted students :

(i) Greater feelings of inferiority.

(ii) Less self-confidence.

(iii) Less perseverance.

(iv) Less of a sense of life goals.

Gowan (1987) has summarized the research findings and concluded that the following factors are related to underachievement :

(i) Lack of clear and definite academic and occupational choice.

(ii) Weak ego control.

(iii) Withdrawal tendency and feelings of self-sufficiency.

(iv) Poor use of time and money.

(v) Neurotic tendencies.

(vi) Authoritaniasm by parents.

(vii) Impossible demands by parents.

(viii) A sense of irresponsibility.

(ix) Lack of self-confidence.

(x) Apathetic view of life.

Gallagher (1960) presents a combination of events which lead to underachievement among children of superior intelligence :

(i) The underachieving child grows up in, or belongs to, a cultural group which does not value education, independence or individual achievement.

(ii) The underachieving child has parents (especially the father) who show limited interest in academic matters or try to put undue pressure on their children to succeed.

(iii) Faced with impossible demands by parents in the home and teachers in the school, the child rejects their programmes.

(iv) The strict and repressive measures of the school turn the chid even more emphatically against the school.

(v) Unable to obtain satisfaction from parental contacts, the child seeks out his peer group for satisfying human relationships. He often finds himself in rebellious and angry groups.

Whitmore (1980) found the following personality and behaviour traits that describe many underachieving gifted children :

(i) A negative self-concept.

(ii) A low self-esteem.

(iii) Expectation of academic and social failure.

(iv) A sense of inability to control or determine outcomes of one's own efforts.

(v) Emotional disturbance.

Most of the factors that lead to underachievement lie outside the school. What can the school do to help the underachieving gifted child? Kirk (1972) suggests the following measures :

(i) Identifying underachieving gifted children during the early years in school.

(ii) Assigning tutors who will support and motivate the children through success in academic fields.

(iii) Counselling parents concerning the problems of the child and better human relations in the family.

(iv) Rewarding the child by praise and recognition in school for efforts and achievements in school work.

(v) Organising small group sessions/special classes for underachieving gifted children with support from specialist teachers.

Whitmore (1980) points out that the creation of a warm, accepting environment can overcome the signs of emotional disturbance of such children. Whitmore (1980) and Butler-Por (1987) have shown that carefully designed programmes, over an extended period of time, can make a positive difference in the academic and social performance of underachievers.

10

Education of Socially Disadvantaged Children

1. Who are the Socially Disadvantaged Children?

In most classrooms there are some children who are socio-culturally deprived, and underprivileged. In recent literature the term socially disadvantaged or simply 'disadvantaged' is used to refer to these children who are economically, educationally, linguistically, or socially disadvantaged. By definition a disadvantaged child is one who —

(i) suffers from a continuing inadequacy of basic necessities of life;

(ii) is subject to detrimental environmental stresses of any kind;

(iii) has been denied the basic and universal rights of children (*i.e.* a stable home; loving mother; a supportive father who provides the material needs, such as protection, clothing, adequate diet, and play space; fresh experience to stimulate language and mental growth; recognition and an encouraging atmosphere, and contact with other children and adults.);

(iv) is at risk of future psycho-educational problems;

(v) is handicapped or disabled because of certain conditions of exogeneous origin (*i.e.* not due to any condition arising out of or within his own body) and

(vi) has been denied the opportunity to grow normally at his own natural rate.

Thus, the term disadvantage refers to an inner condition of a child resulting from an outer deprivation.

2. Causes of Disadvantaged Conditions

The various causes of disadvantaged conditions are as follows :

Economic Causes

Poverty of parents
Mismanagement of money in the home

Poor occupational status of parents
Unemployment, or underemployment
Poor housing
Poor diet
Poor clothing.

Health-related Causes

Malnutrition of children
Inadequate medical care of children
Lack of health care, cleanliness and preventive immunization
Prenatal and post-natal complications.

Home and Neighbourhood factors

Shared, inadequate and crowded home
Lack of play space
Lack of educationally stimulating materials
Depressed or slum-type neighbourhood.

Socio-cultural factors

Defective child-rearing and parenting behaviours
Lack of cultural stimulation
Parental rejection
Over indulgence.

Intellectual Factors

Retarded cognitive growth
Delayed speech
Over or under-stimulation
Educational underachievement,
failure, stagnation and drop-out.

Mental Health factors

Crime and delinquency
Psychiatric problems
Behaviour problems and disorders.

3. Identification of Socially Disadvantaged Children

It is not difficult to identify the socially disadvantaged children. The following check-list of behavioural characteristics is useful for teachers to identify socially disadvantaged children. In addition to the checklist the teacher can examine the school records, interview the parents and children, and if possible pay a visit to their home to confirm his identification.

Identification Checklist for Teachers :

(i) Appears lifeless and incurious.

(ii) Appears deceptively unintelligent.

(iii) Shows a lack of interest; involvement and/or motivation for academic success.

(iv) Has lack of confidence and competence in expressing himself.

(v) Does not participate in classroom discussion.

(vi) Fails to profit from classroom instruction.

(vii) Shows specific learning difficulties in language subject and/or general academic underachievement.

(viii) Shows progressive academic deterioration resulting in failure, repetition of grades and drop-out.

4. Problems of Socially Disadvantaged Children

It is because of their poor social conditions, economic pressures, poor educational backgrounds, differences in language and culture that, for no fault of their own, such children show intellectual, emotional, learning, language and motivational problems. In rural classrooms a teacher (from urban areas) may face an entire class of students socially and culturally different from him. The teacher's inexperience with his students' social conditions puts him at a disadvantaged position. Lack of understanding of the sub-culture's ways and their problems can lead to ineffectiveness of the teacher. Such a teacher is likely to be 'disadvantaged' himself unless he tries to understand his students' problems and take appropriate actions for their education.

Intellectual, Language and Learning Problems of Socially Disadvantaged Children. Socially disadvantaged children are especially handicapped by their basically poor cognitive backgrounds. By the time the child comes to school for formal education his cognitive growth is already depressed. The gap between advantaged and disadvantaged children widens rapidly over increasing years ultimately leading to premature school termination and high rate of stagnation. Such children may have below average intellectual functioning, poor school achievement, low level of aspiration and marginal social occupational adjustment.

Due to infrequent exposure to varied stimulating environmental conditions, disadvantaged children seem to lack adequate perceptual constancy and discrimination. They also lag behind in memory ability and attention span.

The home of the socially disadvantaged children serves in no way to prepare them to equip them with the required readiness to enter the school. This may be because of their poor illiterate parents, apathetic attitude of parents towards education, or backward geographical location of their habitation.

Disadvantaged children and their teachers experience the following difficulties :

(i) Culturally disadvantaged children seem to be generally unaware of the ground rules for success in school work.

(ii) They are less able to learn from being told.

(iii) They are often unable to make simple symbolic interpretations.

(iv) They tend to have small attention span and consequently have difficulty in following directions.

(v) They are unable to use standard language.

(vi) They tend to have little concept of relative size.

(vii) They are less likely to perceive adults as people to whom they can turn for help.

(viii) They seem to have low level of curiosity about the things.

The socially disadvantaged children have language difficulties. Most of them come from families where they are spoken to only when necessary and there is little conversation between parents and their children. Pre-schoolers from such environments tend to have restricted vocabulary, relatively poor articulation, and poor listening discrimination abilities. Their language code pattern is characterized by short, simple and unfamiliar sentences. This combination of language difficulties can handicap the child severely in his school learning for an extended period of time. If such a child cannot understand the teacher's words or interact with others in the classroom because of his language disadvantages he falls behind and loses interest in the tasks of learning.

The socially disadvantaged children have learning difficulties. Such children appear lifeless, incurious, and deceptively unintelligent. They show a lack of interest, involvement, and or motivation for academic success. They lack confidence and competence in expressing themselves. They do not participate in classroom discussions and fail to profit from classroom instructions. They show specific learning difficulties in Language, Mathematics and Science or general academic underachievement. They show progressive academic deterioration or cumulative achievement deficits resulting in high rate of failure, repetition of grade, and premature termination from schooling. The learning problems of socially disadvantaged children are mainly due to depressed cognitive growth and lack of readiness for school education. The intellectual, language, and learning problems of socially disadvantaged children are mainly caused by outer conditions in the home and neighbourhood.

Emotional and Motivational Problems. Emotional development is mostly related to the satisfaction of basic needs of the children. Socially disadvantaged children do possess the same urges and needs as any other child possesses. The socially disadvantaged children have to go without the gratification of their psychological as well as social needs. They do not get the care and attention of their parents as is due to or required by them for their integrated personality development. All the more their participation in child-like activities is also denounced. In most of the cases both the parents being bread earners, these children are left to their own for personal care. The disadvantaged simply receive an ignored and indifferent attitude from their guardians. These children are deprived of any recognization for their praiseworthy acts of achievements. Their queries remain almost unheard and unreplied. Their anxiety to be acquainted with their surrounding is simply suppressed. These children are always on the look out for someone to whom they should love and by whom they should be loved. Virtually they are not given any opportunity to take their own initiative and act at their own free will. Thus, their desire for self-independence is blocked.

Due to immature emotional development, deprivation of stimulation, and lack of opportunity for advancement, disadvantaged children have been drawn to maintain a very low level of motivation which stands in their way for further progress. They do not consider education as a means for upward mobility not because they devalue education, but because they do not expect to rise too far in the occupational world. A majority of disadvantaged adults are found working in the field, on the streets, in construction sites being exploited by contractors and lords. Such children have a preference for immediate reinforcement over delayed reinforcement even when they are assured of greater reward under delayed conditions.

The child's total experience in the unstimulating social environment, poor economic conditions and lack of motivation leave him ill-prepared for the school life. Most of the children come to school in a starved condition. Can you imagine the motivational state of such a starved child sitting idle in the class, looking simply blank, perhaps trying to understand the high sounding ideals and advices presented by the teacher? An unmotivated child not only learns nothing but also creates discipline and learning problems for others. Delinquent tendencies, drop out cases, and other behaviour problems are more frequent among socially disadvantaged children than among others.

5. Educational Programmes for Socially Disadvantaged Children

Socially disadvantaged children are not to be considered as objects who deserve mercy from the society. In general it looks very queer to think in terms of advantages, disadvantages and deprived or privileged children in any enlightened society. Socio-economic policies and programmes are based upon equalities of opportunities in all spheres of life to all irrespective of caste, creed and community. If the disadvantaged children are allowed to remain as such, it simply means keeping the valuable human resources of the society working far below their optimum levels of productivity. That is why developing and progressive societies can ill-afford to keep their potential children underdeveloped or undeveloped. To facilitate the all round development of the socially disadvantaged children will surely pave the way for all round growth of a country. It is callous to be indifferent towards the needs of these children. Moreover, this very attitude ultimately haults the forward march of the society.

The National Policy of Education (1986) — (Programme of Action), has very rightly emphasized systematic efforts directed towards the educational development of such children. What is needed at present is ensuring greater enrolment and retention of such children in the schools, and decrease in their drop out rates. The parents of socially disadvantaged children who themselves are socially disadvantaged require special incentives to allow their children to attend the educational programmes. As it is very true, most of these children add to the income of their family. Thus, monetary compensations to parents along with free educational provisions to the children remain to be the basic requisitions for any successful programme of education for the socially disadvantaged children. The parents have to be convinced about the utility of educating their children.

Development of socially disadvantaged children implies a number of steps :

(i) Understanding the background, needs and problems of such children;

(ii) Change in our attitude towards them;

(iii) Investment on the education of such children; and

(iv) Improvement in their quality of life.

All these are philosophical considerations for the education of such children. What special educational programmes are to be organised so that the disadvantaged children can receive education which are meaningful for them, realise their maximum potentials as individuals, live an adequate and successful life as citizens of the country, and contribute for the forward march of the society?

Special Educational Programmes : Conventional schooling has not been successful in overcoming the problems of the disadvantaged children. The difference between the advantaged and the disadvantaged child, relatively small in size in kindergarten and first grade, becomes larger with each additional school year. The disadvantaged child's deficit becomes cumulative. The disadvantaged child enters school with so much deficiencies and so ill-prepared that initial failures are almost inevitable. When a child enters school with such handicaps and experiences failures, he becomes discouraged and his deficiencies become accentuated. Each year produces increasing frustration and failure. Eventually he becomes alienated from school and seek satisfaction elsewhere.

The first years of school are critical in the child's life. If learning at this time is not successful and satisfying, the child's entire educational career is jeopardised. Repeated failure instils in the child an unsatisfactory self-concept and an antagonistic attitude towards school and learning in general. The special educational programmes for the disadvantaged are designed to develop intellectual and social competencies, positive self-concept, and social attitudes and marketable vocational skills. The principal difference between the programme designed for disadvantaged children and those for the more advantaged is that, in the former many things must be specifically and formally taught whereas more advantaged children are taught these same things in the home and culture as a part of the normal developmental process. Whatever may be the type of educational programmes our objectives should be in conformity with the national priorities :

(i) Increasing enrolment of S.C./S.T. and other disadvantaged children.

(ii) Increasing retention of such children.

(iii) Reducing their rate of drop-outs.

Educational programme for the disadvantaged children includes two main programmes :

Enrichment Activities and

Remedial Programmes.

Enrichment Activities : Enrichment refers to the adaptation of the regular programme to provide educational experiences over and above those provided in the regular programme. It refers to the type of activity devoted to the further development of the particular intellectual skills and talents of the disadvantaged child. In conventional regular programme the disadvantaged child, whether he succeeds or fails, has to adjust to the school and the curriculum. But in enrichment activities the school and the curriculum are to be adjusted to the needs of the child.

Educational programmes for the disadvantaged children should cater to their unique backgrounds, local needs and aspirations. Their unique and fascinating geographical and cultural background, customs and traditions, social vocational life, and the needs and aspiration of the people should be reflected in the curricular and cocurricular activities of the school. This calls for revision of the curriculum, development of special primers through mixed language approach, adopting appropriate methods and using suitable aids.

In the area of intellectual and social competence, enrichment programmes are to be designed to develop and enlarge the child's perceptual and conceptual repertoire and his communicative skills. This typically involves an enrichment of the child's experiences in pre-school centres through local songs, dance, play, stories and conversations. At older age field trips, audio-visual aids, wide reading, cocurricular activities, on-the-job experience, and extra assignments provide additional sources of enriched experiences.

Enriched experiences either in pre-school centres or formal schools will endanger positive attitudes towards self and others, as well as towards the school and other social institution. Such experiences will raise their levels of aspirations and expectations and develop favourable self-images.

Besides these school-based programmes, parent education and functional literacy programmes in non-formal centres, and early intervention programmes mainly for infants and mothers are found effective in enriching the experiences of disadvantaged parents and adults.

Remedial Programmes : Remedial programmes for the socially disadvantaged children refer to two types of activities :

(i) Eliminating ineffective habits and unwholesome attitudes, and reteaching skills which have been incorrectly learned. This refers to remediation of defects.

(ii) Teaching for the first time those habits, skills, and attitudes which have never been learned but should have been and which are needed by such children. This refers to developmental teaching or developing increased competence.

Remedial programmes involve taking a child from where he is and leading him to greater achievement. Remedial teaching is just good teaching concerned with two types of deficiencies — the presence of bad habits and the absence of good habits.

Remedial programmes for the younger disadvantaged are to be mainly of the type of compensatory and preparatory education. Such compensatory and preparatory education can be given through early childhood education and care programmes organised by government agencies or voluntary agencies. The following steps are recommended;

(i) Preventive programmes consisting of health, nutrition, and care.

(ii) Compensatory health, nutritional, educational and social welfare programmes.

(iii) Pre-school education programmes with emphasis on school readiness, Pre-school education for the disadvantaged children should emphasize compensating the deficiencies, remedying the defects, teaching, or developing the essential language and social skills which are prerequisites for entry into the formal school and profiting from educational programmes. The school readiness programme of pre-school education includes all three objectives — compensation, preparation and remediation.

Remedial programmes for the older disadvantaged may include the following activities :

(i) Screening, remediation, and follow-up programmes for learning difficulties of disadvantaged children at different grade points.

(ii) Compensatory and preparatory programmes through non-formal approach.

(iii) Extra classes/special classes, extra coachings, extra time and help for learning difficulties in different subjects.

Telford and Sawrey (1972) suggest three board programmes for the remediation of socially disadvantaged children. These are :

(i) Diminishing the restrictive influences of poverty, discrimination and segregation.

(ii) Providing more and better educational and vocational training programmes.

(iii) Establishing pre-school programmes which intervene early enough in the child's life to have a major effect on the child's perceptual, conceptual, linguistic, and motivational systems.

Appendices

APPENDIX 1

Normal Milestones of Development

SI. No.	Milestone	Age
1.	Smiles at others	4 months
2.	Holds head erect	4 months
3.	Puts objects into mouth	4 months
4.	Rolls from back on to stomach	6 months
5.	Uses hole palm to grasp	7 months
6.	Makes sounds 'anna', 'ad dadda'	7 months
7.	Sits without support	8 months
8.	Responds to name	10 months
9.	Crawls	10 months
10.	Stands by holding on to an object	10 months
11.	Holds object with thumb and index finger	10 months
12.	Stands without support	10 months
13.	Say 'amma', 'Cakka', 'atta', meaningfully	15 months
14.	Walks without support	15 months
15.	Tells own name	18 months
16.	Drinks by self from a glass	21 months
17.	Shows body parts when named	24 months
18.	Indicates toilet needs	24 months
19.	Speaks in small sentences	30 months
20.	Unbuttons clothes	36 months
21.	Gives meaningful verbal answers to simple questions	36 months
22.	Differentiates big and small	36 months
23.	Identifies boy or girl	36 months
24.	Can button clothes	40 months
25.	Combs hair	48 months

We have seen how a normal child develops. Early identification of mental retardation is made by seeing how much a child is delayed on the milestones of development. Identification of mental retardation is done by using certain questionnaires or checklists called screening schedules. Three screening schedules are given below. The first is for the children below 3 years of age. The second is for those between 3-6 years of age. The third is for those aged 7 years and above. In the description of normal milestones of development the mean age of attainment alone is given. However, the age range has to be taken into consideration while screening for developmental delays. Hence, the age range is given in the screening schedule 1.

Screening Schedule No. 1 (Below 3 years)

Sl. No.	Item	Normal age range	Milestone delay if not achieved by
1.	Responds to name/voice	1—3 months	4 months
2.	Smiles at others	1—4 months	6 months
3.	Holds head steady	2—6 months	6 months
4.	Sits without support	5—10 months	12 months
5.	Stands without support	9—14 months	18 months
6.	Walks well	10—20 months	20 months
7.	Talks in 2-3 word sentences	16—30 months	3rd year
8.	Eats/drinks by self	2—3 years	4th year
9.	Tells his name	2—3 years	4th year
10.	Has toilet control	3—4 years	4th year
11.	Avoids simple hazards	3—4 years	4th year
12.	Has fits	Yes	No
13.	Has physical disability	Yes	No

If the child is found to be delayed in any one of the items given from 1—11 and if the child has fits or physical disability suspect mental retardation.

Screening Schedule No. 2 (3 to 6 years)

Observe the following

1. Compared with other children, did the child have any serious delay in sitting, standing, or walking? Yes/No
2. Does the child appear to have difficulty in hearing? Yes/No
3. Does the child have difficulty in seeing? Yes/No

4. When you tell the child to do something, does he seem to have problems in understanding what you are saying? Yes/No
5. Does the child have weakness and/or stiffness in the limbs and/or difficulty in walking or moving his arms? Yes/No
6. Does the child sometimes have fits, become rigid, or lose consciousness? Yes/No
7. Does the child have difficulty in learning to do things like other children of his age? Yes/No
8. Is the child not able to speak at all? (cannot make himself understand in words/say any recognizable words) Yes/No
9. Is the child's speech in any way different from normal (not clear enough to be understood by people other than his immediate family?) Yes/No
10. Compared to other children of his age, does the child appear in any way backward, dull or slow? Yes/No

If any one of the above items in answered 'Yes', suspect mental retardation.

Screening Schedule No. 3 (7 years and above)

1. Compared with other children, did the child have any serious delay in sitting, standing or walking? Yes/No
2. Can the child not do things for himself like eating, dressing, bathing and grooming? Yes/No
3. Does the child have difficulty in understanding when you say "do this or that" ? Yes/No
4. Is the child's speech not clear? Yes/No
5. Does the child have difficulty in expressing without being asked what the child has seen/heard? Yes/No
6. Does the child have weakness and/or stiffness in the limbs and/or difficulty in walking or moving his arms? Yes/No
7. Does the child sometimes have fits, become rigid or lose consciousness? Yes/No
8. Compared to other children of his age, does the child appear in any way backward, dull or slow? Yes/No

If any one of the above items is answered 'yes' suspect mental retardation.

NOTE

In the screening schedules No. 2 and No. 3, there are a number of questions which are overinclusive *i.e.*, those with hearing handicap or physical handicap or epilepsy alone without mental retardation can be spotted. These two screening schedules ensure prompt identification of every single mentally retarded child. Do not worry if the questions sometimes identify persons with handicaps other than mental retardation. Such persons can be assessed later. Our chief concern is identification of mentally retarded children.

Source : NIMH, Secunderabad.

APPENDIX-2

The Persons with Disabilities (Equal Opportunities, Protection of Rights and full Participation) Act, 1995

The Gazette of India : Extra ordinary, Part-II, Section-1 No. 1 of 1996, 1st January, 1996, Ministry of Law, Justice and Company Affairs, New Delhi : Chapter-V Education p. 12-13.

26. The appropriate Governments and the local authorities shall—
    (a) ensure that every child with a disability has access to free education in an appropriate environment till he attains the age of eighteen years;
    (b) endeavour to promote the integration of students with disabilities in the normal schools;
    (c) promote setting up of special schools in Government and private sector for those in need of special education, in such a manner that children with disabilities living in any part of the country have access to such schools;
    (d) endeavour to equip the special schools for children with disabilities with vocational training facilities.
27. The appropriate Governments and the local authorities shall by notification make schemes for—
    (a) conducting part-time classes in respect of children with disabilities who having completed education upto class fifth and could not continue their studies on a whole time basis;
    (b) conducting special part-time classes for providing functional literacy for children in the age-group of sixteen and above;
    (c) imparting non-formal education by untilizing the available manpower in rural areas after giving them appropriate orientation;
    (d) imparting education through open schools or open universities;

(e) conducting class and discussions through interactive electronic or other media;

(f) providing every child with disability free of cost special books and equipment needed for his education.

28. The appropriate Governments shall initiate or cause to be initiated research by official and non-governmental agencies for the purpose of designing and developing new assistive devices, teaching aids, special teaching materials or such other items as are necessary to give a child with disability equal opportunities in education.

29. The appropriate Governments shall set up adequate number of teachers' training institutions and assist the national institutes and other voluntary organisations to develop teachers' training programmes specialising in disabilities so that requisite trained manpower is available for special schools and integrated schools for children with disabilities.

30. Without prejudice to the foregoing provisions, the appropriate Governments shall by notification prepare a comprehensive education scheme which shall make provisions for—

(a) transport facilities to the children with disabilities or in the alternative financial incentives to parents or guardians to enable their children with disabilities to attend schools;

(b) the removal of architectural barriers from schools, colleges or other institutions imparting vocational and professional training;

(c) the supply of books, uniforms and other materials to children with disabilities attending school;

(d) the grant of scholarship to students with disabilities;

(e) setting up of appropriate fora for the redressal of grievances of parents regarding the placement of their children with disabilities.

(f) suitable modification in the examination system to eliminate purely mathematical questions for the benefit of blind students and students with low vision;

(g) restructuring of curriculum for the benefit of children with disabilities;

(h) restructuring the curriculum for the benefit of students with hearing impairment to facilitate them to take only one language as part of their curriculum.

31. All educational institutions shall provide or cause to be provided amanuensis to blind students and students with low vision.

Bibliogarphy

Adhikari, S.D. (1983), "Education of Disadvantaged Children", A paper presented in the Annual Meeting of OIER, Bhubaneswar.

A Teacher's Handbook on IED (1988), NCERT, New Delhi.

Carhart, R., (1970), "Development and Conservation of Speech", in H. Davis and S.R. Silverman (eds.) *Hearing and Deafness*, New York, Holt Rinehart and Winston.

Clark, B. (1988), *From Growing Up Gifted-Developing the Potential of Children at Home and at School* (3rd ed.), Columbus, Merrill.

Dash, M. (1980), "Socially Disadvantaged Children", in *Indian Education*, Volume X, No. 9 and 10, 30-32.

—— (1988), *Educational Psychology*, New Delhi, Deep and Deep Publishers Pvt. Ltd.

—— (1989), *Education of Exceptional Children*, Cuttack, Takshysila.

—— (1993), "The Resource Teacher", In Souvenir of 33rd World Day for the Disabled, OAB, Bhubaneswar.

—— (1996), *Integrated Education for Children with Special Needs*, Puri, Classic Book House.

—— (1998), *Advanced Educational Psychology*, Cuttack, Satyanarayan Book Store.

Educating the Disabled (1987) — Report of a Regional Planning Seminar, Workshop on Special Education, Coimbatore, UNESCO.

"Equal Educational Opportunity for the Disabled", PIED Newsletter, Volume 2, No. 1, 1987, NCERT, New Delhi.

Fry, D.B (1966), "The Development of Phonological System in the Normal and Deaf Child", in F. Smith and G.A. Miller (eds.). *The Genesis of Language : A Psycholinguistic Approach*, Cambridge, Mass, MIT Press.

Furth, H.G. (1961), "Influence of Language on the Development of Concept Formation in Deaf Children", *Journal of Abnormal Social Psychology*, 63, 386—389.

Furth, H.G. (1964), "Research with the Deaf", in *Psychological Bulletin*, 62, 145-164.

Furth, H.G. (1971), "Linguistic Deficiency and Thinking", in *Psychological Bulletin*, 76, 58-72.

Furth, H.G. (1973), Deafness and Learning-A Psychological Approach, Belmany, Wordsworth.

Gowan, J.C. (1957) :, "Dynamics of the Underachievement of Gifted Students", in *Exceptional Chidren*, 24, 98—101.

Hallahan, D.P. and Kaufman, J.M. (1978), *Exceptional Children : Introduction tq Special Education*, New Jersey, Prentice-Hall.

Heward, W.L. and Orlansky, M.D. (1992) : *Exceptional Children* (4th ed.), New York, Macmillan.

Hewett, F.M. and Forness, S.R. (1984), *Education of Exceptional Children*, London, Allyn and Bacon.

Kirk, S. (1962), *Educating Exceptional Children*, Boston, Haughton Mifflin.

Kirk, S., Gallagher, J.S. and Anastasiow, N.J. (1996), *Educating Exceptional Children* (8th Edition), Boston, Houghton Mifflin.

Kough, J. and Dehann, R.F. (1955), "Identifying Children Who Need Help", in *Teacher's Guidance Handbook-1*, Science Research Association, Chicago.

Mental Retardation — A Manual for Multi-Rehabilitation Workers (1988), NIMH, Secunderabad.

Mental Retardation — A Manual for Psychologists (1989), NIMH, Secunderabad.

NCTE Bulletin (1991), Volume III, No. 2—4, NCTE, New Delhi.

National Policy of Education (1986/1992), MHRD, Government of India, New Delhi.

Planning and Management of IED Programme — A Handbook (1987), NCERT, New Delhi.

Programme of Action (NPE, 1992), MHRD, Government of India, New Delhi.

Project Integrated Education for the Disabled (1987), NCERT, New Delhi.

Scheme of Integrated Education for Disabled Children (1987), NCERT, New Delhi.

Source Book for Training Teachers of Hearing Impaired (1987), NCERT, New Delhi.

Source Book for Training Teachers of Visually Impaired (1989), NCERT, New Delhi.

Telford, C.W. and Sawrey, J.M. (1972), *The Exceptional Individual*, London, Prentice Hall.

Williams, C.W. and Hounshell, P.B. (1998), "Enabling the Learning Disabled — Teaching Strategies for Challenged Students", in the *Science Teacher*, January, 1998.

Witty, P. (1955), "Gifted Children — Our Greatest Resource" in *Nursing Outlook*, Volume 3, p. 499.